D0254917

Fort Wallace

A view of Fort Wallace, 1879, from the southeast. The buildings around the parade ground, clockwise from the flagstaff, are guardhouse (stone), enlisted men's barracks (stone), commanding officer's quarters (frame, one and one-half stories), six officers' quarters (frame), adjutant's office (frame), school for children on the post (frame), enlisted men's barracks (stone), enlisted men's barracks (frame), and powder magazine (stone). The remainder of the buildings, clockwise, are two sets of laundresses' quarters (frame), butcher shop (stone, just west of laundresses' quarters), bakery (stone), post chapel and evening school for enlisted men (frame, just off southwest corner of parade ground), commissary storehouse (frame), blacksmith and wheelwright shop (frame), commissary storehouse (frame), granary (frame), quartermaster storehouse (stone, adjacent to granary), building just behind barracks housed kitchen, mess room, and some laundresses' quarters (frame), coal shed (frame), post hospital (stone and frame), building for hospital stewards, hospital kitchen and mess (frame), post trader's store (frame, at far right), kitchen

 'ort **Wallace, Kansas - 1879**
View from South East

and mess room (frame, behind stone barracks), ordnance sergeant's house (frame), two sets of laundresses' quarters (frame), cavalry stable and corral (stone and frame), hay yard (board fence), and mule corral with stalls and wagon shed (frame). Latrines are not shown. Some of these structures had been used for other purposes prior to 1879, and other structures were gone by 1879. For example, one set of laundresses' quarters had served as quarters for the band, when the post had a band. One enlisted men's barracks on the west side of the parade ground was gone by 1879. The artist erred in the placement of the stone barracks on the west. According to ground plans of the post, it stood nearly straight across from the stone barracks on the east and nearer the commanding officer's quarters. The frame barracks on the west had stood nearly straight across from the frame barracks on the east. In 1872 it was converted to a hospital and in 1874 was moved to the location shown in this drawing. Despite minor errors of placement, this is the best composite illustration of Fort Wallace available. None of the structures remains today.

William Harvey Lamb Wallace, 1821–1862. Fort Wallace, Wallace County, and the town of Wallace were named to honor Brigadier General Wallace, who was mortally wounded at the Battle of Shiloh, Tennessee, on April 6, 1862, and died four days later. He was a native of Urbana, Ohio, and moved with his family to Illinois in 1832. He was admitted to the bar in 1846 and the same year volunteered as a private in the First Illinois Regiment to fight in the war with Mexico. He participated in the Battle of Buena Vista and other engagements, rose to the rank of lieutenant, served as regimental adjutant, and returned to Illinois to practice law after the war. In May 1861 he was appointed colonel of the Eleventh Illinois Volunteers. He commanded a brigade at the Battle of Fort Donelson, Tennessee, in February 1862. Because of leadership skills demonstrated there, he was appointed brigadier general of volunteers. At Shiloh he commanded a brigade that withstood the assault of the enemy for six hours and was the last to leave the field. There he was mortally wounded.

Fort Wallace
Sentinel on the Smoky Hill Trail

by Leo E. Oliva

Kansas State Historical Society
Topeka, Kansas

THE AUTHOR: Dr. Leo E. Oliva is a former university professor of history. He farms with his wife, Bonita, in Rooks County, Kansas, and is the owner of Western Books publishing company. In addition Oliva is a freelance historian whose writing and research has focused on the frontier army and Indians as well as local history. This book is the fourth in the Kansas Forts Series; previous titles are *Fort Scott: Courage and Conflict on the Border*, *Fort Hays: Keeping Peace on the Plains*, and *Fort Larned: Guardian of the Santa Fe Trail*. Oliva's other publications include *Soldiers on the Santa Fe Trail* (1967), *Ash Rock and the Stone Church: The History of a Kansas Rural Community* (1983), and *Fort Union and the Frontier Army in the Southwest* (1993).

FRONT COVER: *Farewell*, Fort Wallace, Kansas, 1865–1882, by Jerry D. Thomas. Thomas, a nationally acclaimed artist, has made a career of creating wildlife and western art. His original works will appear on the covers of all eight volumes of the Kansas Forts Series. Thomas is a resident of Manhattan, Kansas.

Fort Wallace: Sentinel on the Smoky Hill Trail is the fourth volume in the Kansas Forts Series published by the Kansas State Historical Society in cooperation with the Kansas Forts Network.

Additional works in the Kansas Forts Series
Fort Scott: Courage and Conflict on the Border
Fort Hays: Keeping Peace on the Plains
Fort Larned: Guardian of the Santa Fe Trail

Copyright © 1998 Kansas State Historical Society

Library of Congress Card Catalog Number 97-81105
ISBN: 0-87726-048-6

Printed by Mennonite Press, Inc., Newton, Kansas

Contents

Foreword

From earliest times the Southern Plains, that vast sweep of the Great Plains and Central Lowland Plains extending southward from the Platte and South Platte Rivers to the Balcones Escarpment in west-central Texas, has had a reputation for violent weather, violent people, and violent history. During the mid-nineteenth century Euro-Americans, their conquest of the eastern United States complete, began to enter the region in large numbers. The war with Mexico and annexation of its northern provinces, the discovery of gold, and finally, thirst for land by a growing immigrant population, laid the groundwork for invasion. Although delayed by the Civil War, the end of that conflict opened the floodgates for an enormous westward movement of people. Predictably the native population resisted the entry into their country by whites, and the struggle for the West began.

The white entrada onto the Plains began first with explorers, hunters, and trappers, and with traders seeking profitable commerce with northern Mexican provinces. These pioneers were followed by the military sent to secure the land for their own people and remove the Indian inhabitants. Military posts sprang up along and in advance of the western frontier of white settlement. Such installations kept the Indians under a semblance of control, and acted as a magnet for white immigration as civilians came first in search of work, and finally as settlers of the land. Often located in advance of railroad construction, some became the nucleus of new towns and cities. Because of this they were pivotal to the development of the West in a far greater sense than simply facilitating its military conquest.

In this brief monograph Leo Oliva has ably encapsulated the story of one such military post—Fort Wallace. Oliva, a careful, meticulous, and highly respected historian, deftly weaves the dramatic story of the Plains Indian country under siege by the irresistible flood tide of white conquest—the tragedy and the triumph of two different cultures in mortal conflict. His broad focus deals with the Indian-white conflict, the building of the fort, the military operations from it, the coming of the railroad, and finally, the abandonment. This fourth volume in the Kansas Forts Series is a well told slice of the history of the conquest of the Western Plains that everyone should enjoy.

W.Y. Chalfant
Hutchinson, Kansas

INTRODUCTION

Fort Wallace was established in 1865 near the Smoky Hill Trail in far western Kansas, a few miles from Colorado Territory, to provide protection from Indians for travelers and a stage line in a vast region. This military outpost was part of a network of frontier forts on the Central Plains arranged to protect overland trails and, later, the construction and operation of railroads.

Initially it was founded to help guard the Smoky Hill Trail from a point 150 miles west of Fort Hays and 200 miles east of Denver. The primary mission was to help prevent Indian resistance to the Anglo-American invasion of prime buffalo country south of the Platte River and north of the Arkansas River.

Military posts were along the Platte and Arkansas at the time, but Fort Wallace was founded in the midst of the largest region of the Central Plains still controlled by several Indian tribes. The troops stationed at Fort Wallace, given the location and missions, faced more Indian opposition and engaged in more battles than those at any other post in Kansas. Even though they faced such opposition, the troops primarily were employed in construction and maintenance of the post, the ubiquitous guard duty, military drill, and occasional scouting duties. Nevertheless, their presence and, especially, the provision of escorts for stagecoaches, wagon trains, and railroad survey and construction crews, and the provision of guard details for stage and railroad stations helped secure an important route of transportation.

The Smoky Hill route included stagecoach and wagon traffic as well as the railroad that replaced them. The soldiers also helped protect settlements that grew along that route and throughout the region. Fort Wallace's officers and soldiers were an important part of the federal government program of overcoming Indian resistance, reducing Indian landholdings, and opening the region for the development of farms and towns. It was part of the expansion of the nation. Indian occupants of the Plains were removed to make way for that development.

1

Plains Indians

Fort Wallace was established and existed because of the presence of Indians whose homelands and hunting grounds had been penetrated by westward-moving miners, farmers, ranchers, merchants, town builders, editors, preachers, lawyers, saloonkeepers, gamblers, whores, outlaws, and the transportation routes they followed. Although overwhelmingly outnumbered and technologically deficient in comparison to the emigrants and the U.S. Army, Indians did not give up their lands and traditional ways of life without a struggle.

From their point of view, they were defending their families, economic base, and culture. To the migrating Euro-Americans who followed the Santa Fe, Oregon, California, Mormon, and Smoky Hill Trails across the Plains, and whose numbers and routes of travel increased greatly after the Civil War when railroads crossed the Plains, Indian resistance was seen as thievery, savagery, and cold-blooded murder.

The emigrants, as they had done since the movement west began in earnest following the creation of the United States in the late eighteenth century, sought aid and protection from the federal government. Virtually everything about federal military policy in the American West was directed to one overwhelming objective: controlling the Indian population. The army was small and poorly funded, but it was charged with the erection of numerous military posts along the routes of travel and in areas of frontier settlement.

1

Hummingbird's camp of Kiowas shows the tipis typical of Plains tribes. Kiowas occasionally hunted and raided north of the Arkansas River.

From those bases of operations, commonly called forts although they were usually not fortifications and possessed few if any defensive works, soldiers were dispatched as needed to face real or imagined Indian threats. Most of their efforts were designed to keep the peace, prevent outrages, and punish offenders. Naturally, this sometimes led to warfare, although engagements were generally sporadic and, with few exceptions, inconsequential.

Several tribes were established in the Central Plains by the nineteenth century. Their resistance to the Euro-American penetration of their lands necessitated the placement of soldiers at Fort Wallace and other posts. Cheyennes, Arapahos, and some bands of Lakota Sioux predominated in present western Kansas, where they periodically were joined by members of the Kiowa, Comanche, Plains Apache (also called Kiowa Apache), and occasionally other tribes.

The buffalo-horse culture of those tribal Americans was a recent development in the long history of people collectively and erroneously known as Indians, whose ancestors had migrated to North America more than ten thousand years before. A succession of cultures periodically had occupied the Central Plains. As some groups migrated from other regions, they pushed out those who had come before.

Pawnee Killer, shown with two of his warriors, was an Oglala Sioux chief who associated with Southern Cheyennes. He was present at the village on Pawnee Fork that was abandoned to General W.S. Hancock in the spring of 1867. He continued to oppose soldiers and travelers in the region and was considered Lieutenant Colonel George Custer's nemesis in Custer's ill-fated campaign during Hancock's War. He reportedly led the warriors who killed Lieutenant Lyman H. Kidder's party on July 1, 1867. He fought at Beecher Island in September 1868 and was at the Battle of Summit Springs in July 1869. He later settled at the Red Cloud Agency, Nebraska.

Spanish, French, Dutch, and English colonists in North America established trade with Indians and introduced new tools, firearms, horses, alcohol, and fatal diseases. Some tribal populations were decimated, and others were pushed into new regions, forcing the inhabitants to relocate. As a result Sioux, Cheyennes, Arapahos, and others moved to the Plains.

Comanches, for example, pushed some Apache bands from the Plains into the Southwest during the sixteenth and seventeenth centuries. A small band of Apaches remained on the Plains and later became closely allied with Kiowas who arrived from the Northern Plains in the eighteenth century. These remnant Apaches were known during the time Fort Wallace was active as Plains Apaches or Kiowa Apaches. The southern bands of Cheyennes and Arapahos arrived in the Central Plains beginning in 1820. They soon faced competition from the westward expansion of the United States.

Bull Bear, a chief of the Cheyenne Dog Soldiers, provided leadership in the resistance to the Euro-American invasion of the buffalo range and land of the Plains tribes. In April 1867 he asked General W.S. Hancock not to move troops near the Cheyenne and Sioux village located on Pawnee Fork, the same village Hancock burned a few days later. Bull Bear was engaged in the warfare along the Smoky Hill Trail that followed. He reportedly tried to protect William Comstock and Abner Sharp Grover when they were killed by Cheyennes in August 1868. Bull Bear was involved in the attack on Forsyth's Scouts at Beecher Island in September 1868. He joined his people on the reservation in present Oklahoma in 1869 but never accommodated himself to reservation life. He returned to the Fort Wallace area to hunt in the early 1870s. He remained on the reservation after the Red River War, 1874–1875.

As these Indians moved onto the Plains and acquired the horse (probably during the first half of the eighteenth century), they gave up agriculture and developed a way of life based on the buffalo, which provided food, shelter, clothing, and spiritual succor. They gave up earth lodges and adapted the mobile tipi for shelter. The horse made the new way of life possible. Plains Indians developed a civilization especially well adapted to the land and its resources.

Black Kettle was a leading peace chief of the Southern Cheyennes. He signed treaties and urged accord with Euro-Americans. It was his village at Sand Creek, Colorado, that was attacked by Colonel John M. Chivington in November 1864. Black Kettle and his wife, as well as many members of his band, died at the Battle of the Washita in November 1868. His life and death exemplified the tragedy of the Plains Indian wars.

Warfare, particularly raiding, became a central feature of Plains' cultures. Courage and bravery in battle became the highest virtues, and men were trained to fight. They were outstanding horsemen and highly skilled at hit-and-run raiding and the decoy-ambush tactic. They were suitably prepared to resist outsiders who penetrated their hunting grounds, especially because they were familiar with the terrain.

English physician William A. Bell was at Fort Wallace in the summer of 1867 and described Indian fighting skills following a battle near the post:

> The Buffalo Indians are probably the finest horsemen in the world. Accustomed from their childhood to chase the buffalo, they live half their time in the saddle. No reins are used to guide their horses, but they press with their heels on whichever side they want to turn. Both hands

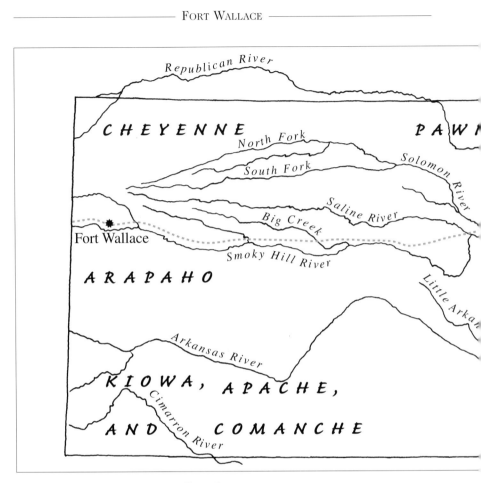

Plains Tribes and the Smoky Hill Trail

and arms are consequently free to use the rifle, the bow, or the spear at pleasure. These men were splendidly armed with rifles for long ranges, bows and arrows for short distances, and spears and tomahawks for hand-to-hand combat.

Gradually some tribes became allies. Kiowas and Comanches shared some of the same territory and eventually stopped fighting each other, especially after Euro-American penetration of the Plains increased. Cheyennes and Arapahos were allies before they reached the Central Plains, and they eventually worked out accommodations with Kiowa and Comanches. Lakota Sioux became friends with Cheyennes and Arapahos.

Together the Plains tribes made a formidable enemy, but their numbers were few in comparison with the population of the growing United

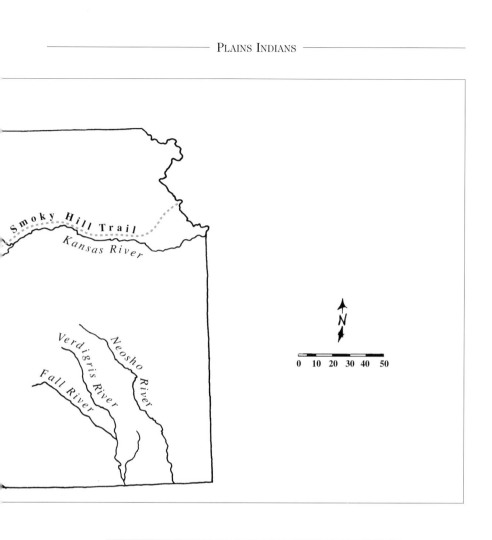

States. The many bands of Sioux, most of whom were on the Northern Plains, constituted the largest of these groups with some twenty thousand people. Only a few hundred of these came regularly to the area of present western Kansas. Some 7,000 Comanches, 2,000 Kiowas, 300 Plains Apaches, 3,500 Cheyennes, and 3,000 Arapahos ranged over the Great Plains.

Comanches, Kiowas, and Plains Apaches were located south of the Arkansas River and came north occasionally to hunt. Southern Cheyennes and Arapahos represented only about half of their two tribes, the remainder living most of the time on the Northern Plains. Thus the Indian population in the region served by Fort Wallace was never more than a few thousand at any one time and usually less. The greater part of each tribe comprised women and children, so the number of adult men available for warfare was not large even when those of several tribes joined together.

Numbers notwithstanding, however, when the tribal way of life on the Plains was threatened, Indians fought back with a vengeance. Major George A. Forsyth, who led a special unit at the Battle of Beecher Island in 1868, declared these tribesmen to be "the wildest and most fierce and warlike of all the Indians of the Great Plains." The Indians, undoubtedly, would have considered that a compliment.

These tribal Americans hunted buffalo throughout the region and encamped along the Republican, Solomon, Saline, and Smoky Hill Rivers, and other streams and tributaries. Some places were considered sacred and some were scenes for ceremonial celebrations. When they resisted Euro-American intruders, Plains tribes not only were protecting their homeland but were fighting for their entire way of life.

Indian-white relations on the Plains deteriorated dramatically during the Civil War, and Indian resistance along routes of travel became intense. The perennial problem of determining who of the tribesmen were hostile and who were friendly produced fatal consequences in November 1864. Colonel John M. Chivington and his Third Colorado Cavalry attacked a Cheyenne and Arapaho encampment under Black Kettle, a Cheyenne peace chief, at Sand Creek in eastern Colorado Territory some forty miles north of Fort Lyon on the Arkansas River.

The Sand Creek Massacre increased tension throughout the Plains (although this atrocity was condemned by government officials). The following year, in 1865, a few leaders of the tribes who claimed western Kansas as their homeland accepted the terms of the treaties of the Little Arkansas, by which they agreed to leave their homelands and settle on assigned reservations south of the Arkansas River.

Many tribal leaders, however, neither signed nor accepted the terms of these agreements. These factions, of which the Cheyenne Dog Soldiers were best known, vowed to fight to retain their lands and continued to oppose westward migration at nearly every opportunity. They were eventually crushed into submission by the army and the onrush of Euro-Americans who built railroads, slaughtered the buffalo, and established towns, ranches, and farms. Fort Wallace, located on the Smoky Hill Trail, was a part of that conquest.

2

The Smoky Hill Trail

T he Smoky Hill Trail, named for the Smoky Hill River, which it followed for some distance, joined Missouri River towns such as Atchison and Leavenworth, Kansas, with Denver, which was located near mining camps in what became Colorado Territory (it was Kansas Territory until 1861). This trail, when opened for travel in 1859, was the shortest route between the Missouri valley and the Rocky Mountain mining camps.

The Smoky Hill River runs nearly six hundred miles from its source in eastern Colorado to its junction with the Republican River at present Junction City, Kansas, to form the Kansas River, an important tributary of the Missouri River, at Kansas City. A route along the Smoky Hill valley was well known to Indians, who followed the water supply and found good hunting among the buffalo herds and other game that abounded in the region. A large grove of cottonwood trees along the river near the present Kansas and Colorado border was an important camping site for Plains Indians and later for Euro-American travelers. The Smoky Hill River was explored in 1844 by John C. Fremont of the U.S. topographical engineers, but it was not an important trail for citizens of the United States until the Colorado gold rush of 1859.

The major overland routes across the Central Plains had been the Santa Fe Trail along the Arkansas valley to the south and the Oregon-California Trail along the Platte valley to the north. It was possible to follow either of these to the new mining camps in present Colorado, but a

Departure from Atchison *by Theodore R. Davis, from* Harper's New Monthly Magazine, *July 1867. The Butterfield Overland Despatch and its successors followed the Smoky Hill Trail across western Kansas and eastern Colorado Territory to Denver.*

road along the Smoky Hill valley was shorter by approximately one hundred miles. Another route was laid out north of the Smoky Hill across northern Kansas by the Leavenworth and Pike's Peak Express, but it soon was abandoned in favor of the Platte River road.

Boosters in several Missouri River towns touted the Smoky Hill route, and several guidebooks were published without benefit of investigating the route. Those who attempted to follow this "trail" discovered it only existed on paper. Some became lost, and others nearly perished. In one party several men starved to death. The proposed trail along the Smoky Hill fell into disrepute, and some called it the starvation trail. The route needed a thorough exploration.

To assist those using this route, William Green Russell led a thirty-six-man survey team from Leavenworth to Denver early in 1860 to prepare a map and guide to the trail. They reported favorably on the availability of water and grass and noted the presence of wood at some potential campsites. Where firewood was not always available, buffalo chips could be used as fuel. The major obstacle to the use of this route was Indians. With this favorable report, the boosters decided a road

Overland Coach Office, Denver City *by Theodore R. Davis,* Harper's Weekly, *January 1, 1866. Denver was the western terminus of the Smoky Hill Trail. The words "Overland Despatch" appear at the top of the building on the left.*

should be laid out, camping sites identified, and stream crossings improved.

In June 1860 H. T. Green of Leavenworth conducted a twenty-nine-man survey party over the route, taking time to improve stream crossings and locate favorable campsites. Green recommended that travelers going to the Colorado mines follow this route, which was not only easy to negotiate but also nearly one hundred miles, and therefore several days, shorter than either the Arkansas or Platte routes. He noted that the longest distance between water sources was only twenty-two miles. He was either unaware of or discounted Indian threats to travelers.

The Civil War interrupted plans for developing this road along the Smoky Hill River, and little was done until 1865 when David A. Butterfield, a former Denver businessman who resided in Atchison, Kansas, prepared to open a freight and stagecoach business over the Smoky Hill Trail. In designing this enterprise, which began operations as the Butterfield Overland Despatch (commonly known as the BOD), Butterfield requested military assistance. In June 1865 Major General Grenville M. Dodge, commanding the Department of the Missouri at Fort

Theodore R. Davis, self-portrait, 1867. Davis was a news correspondent and artist for Harper's publications and others during and after the Civil War. He traveled the Smoky Hill Trail in 1865 and in 1867 reported on military activities on the Plains, including Fort Wallace, during the Hancock expedition. His reports and illustrations were important sources of information about the frontier for eastern readers.

Leavenworth, sent Second Lieutenant Julian R. Fitch of the U.S. Signal Corps to survey the Smoky Hill route. Lieutenant Fitch led a survey team and construction crew, headed by Isaac E. Eaton, over this route during June, July, and August, to locate and establish stage stations at intervals of approximately twelve miles. The survey was escorted by 250 troops.

Theodore R. Davis labeled this "Pond Creek," but no bluffs like those shown are near that stream. The bluffs south of the Smoky Hill River, where the army first established Camp Pond Creek in 1865, are not as prominent either. This may be an example of artistic license in which bluffs from another point on the Smoky Hill Trail were "moved" to provide the background for the wagon train. Perhaps it was a scene at another location along the Smoky Hill that was misnamed. The sketch appeared in Harper's New Monthly Magazine, *July 1867.*

This came at a time of increased Indian resistance on the Plains, and the army was called upon for additional protection.

The survey party encountered no Indians, perhaps because of the presence of the troops. Fitch noted the absence of Indians and declared that "the advantages of the Smoky Hill route over the Platte and Arkansas must be apparent to everybody." It was shorter, had more water, timber, buffalo chips, and grass, did not have long stretches of sand to pass through as did the other routes, and had several good places to locate military posts. It was presumed that military protection would be an essential ingredient of a successful stagecoach operation along the route.

Eaton was equally impressed with the potential of this trail and declared "the roadbed itself is the best natural one I have ever seen, and

I fail to do the Smoky Hill route justice when I say it is 100 per cent superior to either the Platte or Arkansas routes in every respect." By September 1865 the Butterfield Overland Despatch had established stations and distributed 250 mules to assist with daily coach service that started that month. Military protection also was on the way.

The BOD began freighting operations in June 1865, and stagecoach service began in September. The stations along the way were still being constructed and stocked when the first stagecoach left Atchison on September 11, 1865, with Butterfield as a passenger. It arrived in Denver on September 23. Coaches soon left Atchison and Denver each day for the trip. The one-way fare was $175 per person; it included no meals, which had to be purchased along the way, and baggage was limited to forty pounds.

Although the survey party and construction crews encountered no Indian resistance, Indians began raiding the stage stations soon after service began. They occasionally threatened a coach. In early October 1865 a party of about thirty Indians attacked a BOD coach near Monument Station. The passengers defended the coach as long as possible before abandoning it to the Indians and escaping on the mules to Carlyle Station to the east. The Indians looted the coach and burned it.

Butterfield, realizing that the success of his line depended on safety, requested military assistance. The army responded with several new forts where their garrisons could provide escorts and guard stage stations. One of these posts was located near Pond Creek Station, part of the army's network designed to protect the route.

The stage station erected in September 1865 at Pond Creek, a tributary of the Smoky Hill River, became the focus for a military camp that became Fort Wallace. Theodore Davis, a reporter and artist for *Harper's New Monthly Magazine,* traveled the Smoky Hill Trail on a BOD coach in November 1865. He described Pond Creek as "the most picturesque station on the route. The creek comes out of the plains near a fine cottonwood grove, runs with a considerable current for five or six miles, and sinks into the plains."

William A. Bell, an Englishman who traveled the route in 1867, also described Pond Creek Station:

> Standing side by side, and built of wood and stone, are the stables and the ranche in which the drivers and ostlers live. Behind is a coralle, or yard, divided off from the plain by a wall of stones. In this is kept the hay, &c., belonging to the station. A little subterranean passage, about five feet by three, leads from the stables to the house. Another one leads

from the stables to a pit dug in the ground, about ten yards distant. This pit is about eight or ten feet square, is roofed with stone supported on wood, and just on a level with the ground portholes open on all sides. . . . Another narrow subterranean passage leads from the house to a second pit, commanding the other side of the station; while a third passage runs from the coralle to a larger pit, commanding the rear. In both houses, many repeating Spencer and Henry breech-loading rifles—the former carrying seven, and the latter eighteen charges—lie loaded and ready. . . . When attacked the men creep into these pits, and, thus, protected, keep up a tremendous fire through the portholes. Two or three men, with a couple of breech-loaders each, are a match for almost any number of assailants. . . . The Indians are beginning to understand the covered rifle pits, and the more they know of them the more careful they are to keep at a respectful distance from them.

Although the employees at each stage station were expected to defend their positions, if possible, the Butterfield Overland Despatch and its customers expected the army to keep Indians under control. Shortly three new military posts were established to help protect the Smoky Hill Trail, and additional troops were sent during times of crisis.

3

Military Service

The military was assigned the arduous task of subduing Indians and opening their lands for exploitation and development. This mission was complicated by citizens demanding protection, a jingoist press demanding Indian removal or annihilation, and a government demanding results for little expense. Although chronically understaffed and inadequately outfitted for the task, the military eventually handled the nation's "Indian problem."

Little honor but much hardship accompanied military service on the frontier. Low pay, poor living conditions, and oppressive discipline made recruiting and keeping competent soldiers difficult. Most regiments were rarely filled to authorized capacity, and desertion was a perennial problem in the West. In most years more than 10 percent of the enlisted men in the entire army, in some years more than 20 percent, deserted. Some regiments lost more than 50 percent of those enlisted for five years before their term of service expired.

After the Civil War a parsimonious Congress reduced the military budget to a level insufficient for fundamental activities. The authorized strength of the army quickly fell to fifty-seven thousand in 1866 and to twenty-five thousand by 1874. Most companies operated with fewer than the authorized number of enlisted men. In 1881, for example, cavalry regiments averaged 82 percent of authorized strength and the infantry averaged 85 percent, including the sick, prisoners, and others unfit for duty. Some infantry companies did not have twenty-five men available for duty.

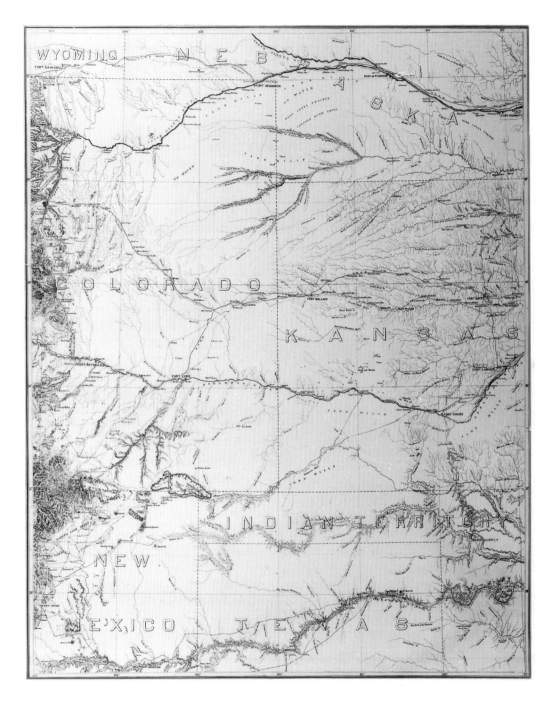

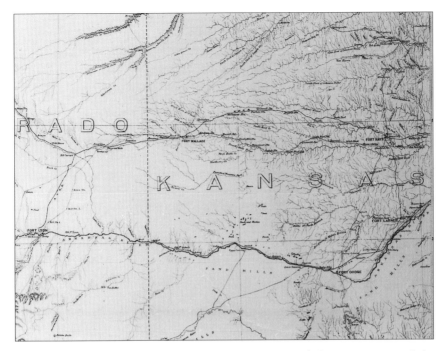

Detail from map on facing page showing the area of the Department of the Missouri, 1873.

The provisions, clothing, and equipment remaining from the Civil War, regardless of condition, were issued to troops for the next decade. Sometimes ammunition was so limited that enlisted men had no target practice. Soldiers' basic dress included woolen trousers, shirts, blouses, socks, long underwear, forage caps, and campaign hats, as well as shoes for the infantry or boots for the cavalry. Footwear was poorly constructed and did not fit the shape of many soldiers' feet. Most clothing issued required modifications before it fit each man. Each company usually had a soldier who performed the duties of tailor in his spare time.

The base pay for privates at the end of the Civil War was sixteen dollars per month, which was reduced to thirteen dollars in 1870. This resulted in increased desertions, and more than 32 percent of all enlisted men deserted in 1871. The rate remained high for several years. Some soldiers had little desire to risk their lives for the compensation provided.

Such limited manpower and supplies made it difficult for the army to supress Indian resistance on the Plains after the Civil War. Federal policy toward Indians was further tangled because authority over Indian affairs had been divided since 1849 between the U.S. Army in the War Department and the Bureau of Indian Affairs in the Department of the Interior. Both soldiers and Indians were perplexed as government policy alternated between the use of force and peaceful negotiations.

Indians were not of one mind, either. Individuals and groups in various tribes wanted accommodation and peace while others of the same tribes favored war. Soldiers often were frustrated in their attempts to deal directly with the tribes because distinguishing between peaceful and hostile individuals frequently was impossible. Hostile Indians practiced a form of hit-and-run warfare that made it virtually impossible to locate and punish the offenders. When the innocent were punished for brazen acts of violence or intimidation, the flames of warfare were fanned higher.

Soldiers also were impeded by the Indians' knowledge of the land, enabling them to strike and disappear before troops could find them. One officer described these natives as being everywhere and yet nowhere, meaning they seemed to strike without warning and melt away before any effective opposition could be mounted. As Captain Albert Barnitz, with the Seventh Cavalry at Fort Wallace, explained in an August 1867 letter to his wife: "When you go after Indians in any force they of course run away from you if they can, and they always can unless you are able to move very rapidly, and know just where they are."

Although the army was sent to deal with Indian problems, using force as necessary, civilian leaders and officials from the Bureau of Indian Affairs sought agreement short of warfare. Thus, periodically, peace councils were conducted and treaties were signed. During those times the army was held in check, until conflict occurred again.

United States citizens wanted to gain access to Indian lands, through treaties if possible and by warfare if necessary. The Indians, on the other hand, wanted protection from the trespassers who killed buffalo, cut trees, used water holes and campgrounds, and tried to keep them away from routes of travel and white settlements. Treaty negotiations, like all Indian-white relations, were conducted in an atmosphere of distrust, for neither side understood the culture of the other nor believed the other would abide by an agreement. Thus, eventually, all treaties were broken by one or both sides, and the army was directed to use force to remove Indians to assigned reservations where they could be controlled.

The army was governed by orders from the top down, and it was administered through a geographical arrangement of military divisions and departments. At the close of the Civil War military posts of Kansas, including Fort Wallace, along with posts in other nearby states and territories, were within the Department of the Missouri. Command and supply were coordinated at Fort Leavenworth on the Missouri River. Several regiments of infantry and cavalry were distributed among numerous posts and shifted as the situation demanded. In 1865 some of these soldiers were assigned to duty on the Smoky Hill Trail.

4

The Founding of Fort Wallace

As the Civil War ended and Indian threats to overland travel across the Plains grew more audacious, military leaders attempted to provide the protection that citizens demanded. Plans for developing the Smoky Hill Trail resulted in additional military posts along the route west of Fort Riley, including Forts Harker (originally Fort Ellsworth), Hays (originally Fort Fletcher), Monument (near Monument Station), and Wallace (originally Camp Pond Creek) as well as small temporary encampments at or near other stage and, later, railroad stations. Fort Ellsworth, which became Fort Harker, had been established in 1864 to help protect the military road between Fort Riley and newly established Fort Zarah on the Santa Fe Trail east of present Great Bend, Kansas. Harker was situated on the Smoky Hill route and became part of the chain of posts along that road in 1865. Fort Wallace, the westernmost post in Kansas, was responsible for a vast territory occupied by several Indian tribes.

Soon after Lieutenant Julian Fitch completed the survey of the Smoky Hill route and the BOD began operation, General Grenville M. Dodge, who was replaced as department commander by Major General John Pope, investigated conditions along the Smoky Hill and Arkansas routes. After observing and reviewing Indian threats to overland travel, Dodge recommended that troops be placed at several points along the Smoky Hill Trail west of Fort Harker to protect the BOD and other travelers, guard stage stations, and escort stagecoaches as needed. Along the Smoky Hill Trail he selected sites at Big Creek (which became Fort

General Grenville M. Dodge selected the site for the location of Fort Wallace on the Smoky Hill Trail.

Fletcher, later Fort Hays), Monument Station (which was abandoned within two years), and Pond Creek (which became Fort Wallace).

On October 26, 1865, General William T. Sherman ordered a post established near Pond Creek Station of the BOD, originally known as Camp Pond Creek. It was named Fort Wallace the following year to honor

In the fall of 1865 Indians attacked or threatened several stations along the Smoky Hill Trail including Downer's Station in present Trego County. This 1867 sketch of Downer's Station is by Private Ado Hunnius, Company D, Third Infantry.

Brigadier General William Harvey Lamb Wallace who died April 10, 1862, of wounds received at the Battle of Shiloh, Tennessee.

Pond Creek, a northern tributary into the Smoky Hill River, was named for Major James Burton Pond, Third Wisconsin Cavalry, who had commanded two companies of his regiment on escort duty for the survey of the Smoky Hill route in the summer of 1865. The escort also had included two companies of Thirteenth Missouri Cavalry, commanded by Captain D. C. McMichael and Captain J. W. C. Schnell. When the military camp was established near Pond Creek Station later that year, Captain McMichael commanded the camp and garrisoned it with troops of his regiment.

The exact date of the founding of this camp has not been determined, but Captain McMichael and his troops were there by late November 1865. On November 19, as these troops were marching from Fort Harker to the new camp, Indians attacked Downer's Station some ninety miles to the east. They killed three men and burned the stagecoach at the station. On November 22 Indians threatened a stagecoach leaving Chalk Bluff Station, some thirty miles west of Downer's Station, but this coach was escorted by troops and eluded the attackers. Because the garrison that

Captain Theophilus H. Turner was acting assistant surgeon at Fort Wallace from June 1866 until his sudden death from acute gastritis at the post on July 27, 1869. A dedicated medical officer, Turner also is recognized by the scientific community for his discovery, only a few miles from Fort Wallace, of the nearly perfect fossil remains of the Elasmosaurus platyurus. *"Dr. Turner's dragon" was part of the Academy of National Sciences' 1986 exhibit* Discovering Dinosaurs.

headed for Camp Pond Creek was not far from the scene of violence, they may have formed part of the escort. On November 27, 1865, the commanding officer at Monument Station was ordered to send two-thirds of its commissary stores to Pond Creek. This was apparently to be the garrison's winter food supply.

The initial site of Camp Pond Creek was on the bluffs south of the river, across from and approximately two miles east of Pond Creek Station. There troops constructed dugouts for their winter quarters. Also, during December 1865 a military road was surveyed from Pond Creek to Fort Lyon in Colorado Territory. Later, routes were also laid out to Fort Dodge and Fort Larned in Kansas. The post was connected by the Smoky Hill Trail with Denver to the west and Forts Hays, Harker, and Riley to the east.

Despite these connections, the garrison believed or claimed their food supply was nearly exhausted by February 1866. Although the commissary was not bare, troops at Camp Pond Creek feared starvation and abandoned the post on February 14, 1866. They had no way of knowing that supplies that would have "saved the garrison" were en route. The term of enlistment for the volunteer troops was about to expire, and they may have used the depleted commissary as an excuse to head for Fort Leavenworth to be mus-

George A. Armes was post adjutant at Fort Wallace during July 1866 when he was a second lieutenant in the Second Cavalry. A Civil War veteran with the brevet rank of major, Armes was promoted to captain in the Tenth Cavalry (a unit of buffalo soldiers) before he had served one month at Wallace. The following year, when stationed at Fort Hays, Armes led Tenth cavalrymen in two important engagements with Indians, one near the Saline River and the other near Prairie Dog Creek. He was wounded in the first of those battles. His autobiography, Ups and Downs of an Army Officer (1900), provides insight into the frontier army.

tered out of service. According to the post's surgeon, "the post was abandoned with a comparatively large amount of stores."

Both food and replacement troops were soon on the way from Fort Fletcher to reoccupy Camp Pond Creek. Captain Edward Ball and his Company H, Second Cavalry, arrived on March 8, 1866. They did not move into the dugouts abandoned by the first garrison but established a new camp north of the river and nearer to Pond Creek Station, perhaps one-half mile to the east. This garrison comprised Captain Ball, Lieutenant Patrick W. Harrigan (who served as quartermaster and commissary officer), Surgeon W. H. Forwood, and forty-seven enlisted men.

This was a temporary arrangement. Supplies for Fort Wallace were shipped four hundred miles from the quartermaster and commissary depots at Fort Leavenworth. Communication, until the arrival of the telegraph at the post in late 1869, was by daily stagecoach service in each direction, connecting to the east with the railroad building westward across Kansas. The railroad reached the nearby town of Wallace in late 1869.

On April 1, 1866, Company I, First U.S. Volunteer Infantry, joined the garrison. This company transferred to Fort Fletcher on April 29. An official order issued by General Pope, Department of the Missouri, on April 18, 1866, named this post Fort Wallace, and the camp received that information on April 23. Although this designation was permanent, the garrison and location were not.

In May 1866 Company B, Sixth U.S. Volunteer Infantry, and Company M, Second Cavalry, arrived, the former coming from Fort Kearney, Nebraska Territory, and the latter from Fort Lyon, Colorado Territory. Captain Ball and Company H, Second Cavalry, and Surgeon Forwood, were transferred to Fort Larned. Captain James J. Gordon, Sixth Volunteer Infantry, became post commander with ninety officers and men. In June they were joined by Surgeon Theophilus H. Turner, who served at the post until his death in July 1869. Bayard Taylor, a reporter for the *New York Tribune,* traveled west by stagecoach over the Smoky Hill Trail in June 1866. In his article about the trip he noted that at Pond Creek "there is a new military post called Fort Wallace." Unfortunately, he provided no description.

When Captain Gordon's term of service expired he passed command to Lieutenant Alfred E. Bates, Second Cavalry, on July 5. Second Lieutenant George A. Armes, Second Cavalry, arrived during the month and became post adjutant. Bates selected the permanent site for Fort Wallace, approximately two miles east of the camp and north of the river (in what is now the northeast quarter of section 29, township 13 south, range 38 west). This high ground on the Smoky Hill Trail offered a view for several miles up and down the river valley.

5

Building Fort Wallace

Fort Wallace was designed to accommodate four companies of troops, four hundred men, but it was usually garrisoned by fewer troops. Troops began constructing stone buildings and opened at least two stone quarries about three miles southeast of the post, where they dressed the limestone before hauling it to the construction site. A road with a river crossing led from the post to the quarries. A stone corral near one quarry protected the draft animals that hauled the stone to the post. Some logs for the buildings were hauled from the Republican River, one hundred miles to the north.

A post surgeon noted that when construction began Fort Wallace "was rather an encampment than a post." The soldiers "had passed the previous winter in an uncomfortable manner for the want of proper shelter," he continued, "and the extent to which they profited by that experience may be judged by the zeal and industry with which they commenced and continued to work as they thought for their own benefit the coming winter." He also explained that soldiers did most of the construction, "and that in connection with the duties required of Soldiers at an isolated post in a wild indian country far from its base of supplies, an amount of work rarely exceeded by a command whose average strength was little above one hundred."

Construction paused when Company M, Second Cavalry, left in September 1866, until the arrival of Company E, Third Infantry, the following month. A post surgeon explained that the men of the Sixth Volunteer

29

Fort Wallace, June 1867, Harper's Weekly, *July 27, 1867.*

Infantry who remained during that interval, and "whose hourly expectation of their Muster out dispelled all interest in the improvements already begun," did nothing until the arrival of Company E, Third Infantry."

Then work on the barracks was pushed rapidly, wrote the surgeon, because of the "approach of winter with all its known severity in this region." In the rush, he noted, was "a disregard of suggestions as to the necessity of light, space and ventilation for the purpose of health." He lamented the absence of "sufficient regard to those principles in the construction of Barracks so essential to the comfort and well being of those who should occupy them." Even so, soldiers welcomed the shelter when snow arrived to interrupt their construction efforts.

The first set of barracks was completed in December 1866, and a company of infantry and a portion of a cavalry troop were in residence by Christmas. The remainder of the garrison remained in tents, which some soldiers preferred over the doorless barracks. Company kitchens and mess areas also were housed in tents. Some soldiers welcomed escort and scouting duties because these provided relief from the poor living conditions at the post.

When Captain Albert Barnitz, Seventh Cavalry, arrived at Fort Wallace in June 1867, he found "five large buildings (of stone) have been completed here, and others are under way. Those finished are the Suttler's Store, commissary building, one company's quarters, a citizens and officer's mess house. The officers all live in tents, or board buildings at present." He described the stone quarry and noted that "the stone is of a yellowish hue—somewhat variegated, sprinkled with red and brown though some of the blocks are nearly white. It is very soft when first quarried, and is dressed with carpenter's tools! They actually saw it up into blocks of the proper size, and then plane it with an ordinary jack plane!—but it soon hardens, and resists the weather admirably."

Work continued on the post buildings for several years, with more than forty structures completed, some of stone and others frame, the lumber hauled to the post by wagon train from the westward-building railroad. The railroad reached Fort Riley in 1866 and extended to Ellsworth and Hays City the following year. In 1868 the line was completed to Sheridan, fifteen miles east of Fort Wallace. A year-long hiatus followed, during which the financially strapped rail company was reorganized and became the Kansas Pacific Railway.

The 234-mile track from Sheridan to Denver was completed in August 1870. The town of Wallace, near the northwest corner of the military reservation, was a division point on the line and provided the station for supplies coming to Fort Wallace.

Total construction costs for the 639-mile Kansas Pacific system was $34,357,491. Even with the grant of 6,273,910 acres (291,968.57 acres in Wallace County), federal subsidies, and business generated by the railroad, the Kansas Pacific was unable to cover the cost of construction plus interest, was placed in receivership in 1876, and consolidated with the Union Pacific Railway in 1880. The sale of the land-grant holdings in Wallace County began in 1868 and continued until 1925. The railroad, dependent on military protection, was always an important link in the shipment of supplies and construction materials to Fort Wallace.

31

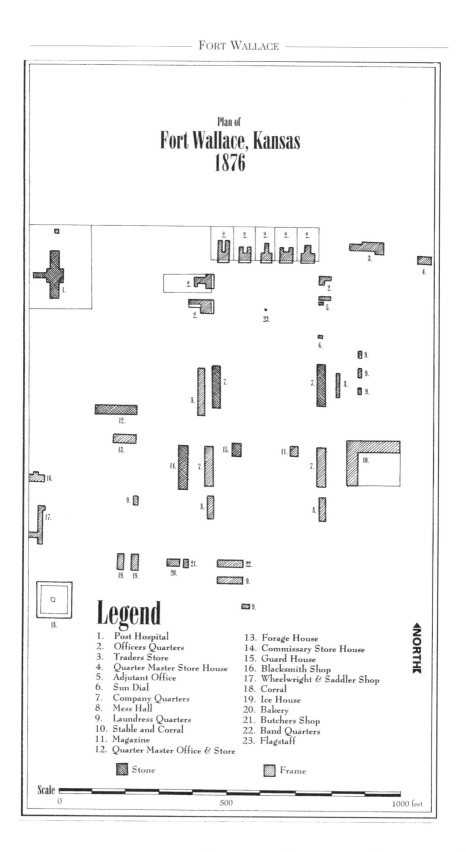

Plan of
Fort Wallace, Kansas
1876

Legend

1. Post Hospital
2. Officers Quarters
3. Traders Store
4. Quarter Master Store House
5. Adjutant Office
6. Sun Dial
7. Company Quarters
8. Mess Hall
9. Laundress Quarters
10. Stable and Corral
11. Magazine
12. Quarter Master Office & Store

13. Forage House
14. Commissary Store House
15. Guard House
16. Blacksmith Shop
17. Wheelwright & Saddler Shop
18. Corral
19. Ice House
20. Bakery
21. Butchers Shop
22. Band Quarters
23. Flagstaff

Stone   Frame

▲NORTH

Scale
0   500   1000 feet

Enlisted men's barracks, Fort Wallace, July 15, 1868, when the garrison comprised Companies B, C, and I, Fifth Infantry. Some members of these companies are in the photograph. This was one of two stone barracks. From descriptions and other photographs, this building was on the east side of the parade ground and faced west.

While the railroad helped transport materials to Fort Wallace, civilian employees assisted the troops in the construction of many post buildings. In September 1866, when Lieutenant R. E. Flood, Sixth Volunteer Infantry, was commanding officer, civilian employees were hired to assist the garrison. An unidentified guide and interpreter was paid one hundred dollars per month, a chief carpenter six dollars per day, three carpenters four dollars per day, two stonemasons ninety dollars per month, and eight stonemasons four dollars per day. The following month a civilian blacksmith was added at one hundred dollars per month. Lieutenant Joseph Hale, Third Infantry, commanded the post, and Second Lieutenant Frederick H. Beecher, Third Infantry, commissary officer and quartermaster, supervised construction.

During the autumn the stores, property, and the garrison moved to the new site as construction continued. Many soldiers continued to live in tents. Work on buildings slowed during the winter months, but construction efforts intensified as soon a spring weather permitted in 1867. A second barracks was completed, a post surgeon observed, "with some improvements but with most of the imperfections of the other that was erected."

Fort Wallace officers' quarters, looking northwest across the parade ground. The one and one-half story house at the left was home for the commanding officer. Of the six other officers' quarters, three and a portion of a fourth are shown. The other two were located to the right, off the photo. All were frame structures.

Fort Wallace officers' quarters, July 15, 1868, looking northeast. These quarters were on the north side of the parade ground.

34

Fort Wallace officers' quarters, about 1868, looking toward the northeast corner of the parade ground. The three buildings on the left were on the north side of the parade ground, and the two on the right were on the east side. In the 1870s the two on the right were used as the post adjutant's office and the school for children at the post. The structure in the background at far right was the post trader's store.

Both stone barracks, one located on the east side of the parade ground and the other on the west side, were 118 by 25 feet, with walls two feet thick. Each building was divided into soldiers' quarters, one hundred feet long, with two rooms at the end for the first sergeant's quarters and a storeroom. The quarters were lighted by three large windows on the west and two on the east. The upper part of each door was glass. The barracks were heated by wood-burning stoves. The quarters in each building contained forty double bunks to accommodate eighty men. Kitchens and mess rooms were in detached frame structures.

Other buildings completed during the summer and fall of 1867 included a quartermaster and commissary storehouse of lumber, 120 by 30 feet, a stone bake house, a stone stable, and stone officers' quarters. A large tent, erected at the new site before any permanent structures were built, served as the post hospital until a frame hospital was constructed (work on the new hospital began in 1867, but it was not completed for several years).

Quartermaster storehouse, Fort Wallace, July 15, 1868.

During 1867 an eight-foot dam was constructed across the Smoky Hill River to assure a reliable supply of water and ice. The number of civilian employees increased, peaking at 215 in January 1869. They included laborers, teamsters, clerks, saddlers, wagon masters, herders, packers, wheelwrights, plasterers, painters, and quarrymen. The 1870 federal census listed 286 soldiers and 168 civilians in the Fort Wallace vicinity. Many civilians were employed at the post, just as they had been during the years of construction.

In November 1867 General Philip H. Sheridan, department commander, directed that stone for buildings not to be dressed but laid up rough, and that all buildings be completed in a plain manner, as economically as possible. Construction of many posts in the department at the same time and the limited military budget precluded any extravagance or waste.

Later two frame barracks were constructed, similar to the stone buildings but a few feet longer and equipped with bathrooms. A row of officers' quarters formed the north side of the parade ground, while the guardhouse and a magazine were on the south. Each set of officers' quarters was forty by twenty feet, frame construction, with a veranda across the front. Each building, except the commanding officer's quarters, was divided into two sets of quarters, each comprising three rooms on either side of the central hall. Some of these buildings had kitchens added to the

View of Fort Wallace in the 1870s. The post, as described by several visitors, appeared like a small village on the Plains.

Looking southwest from the Fort Wallace parade ground in the 1880s. Structures from left to right are the guardhouse; portion of laundresses' quarters behind; commissary storehouse; enlisted men's barracks; portion of building behind the barracks that served as kitchen, mess, and quarters for laundresses; and the quartermaster storehouse on the right.

rear and each had a privy in the back yard. Officers' row had a board fence behind and a picket fence in front.

The stone guardhouse, thirty-four by thirty-one feet with a veranda, contained a central hall, sergeant's room, five small cells, a guardroom, and a prisoners' room. The post surgeon noted that this building was often crowded. Two stone storehouses, 124 by 24 feet, each with a cellar were lighted with skylights. A grain house of lumber had capacity of fifteen thousand bushels. No description was found of the first bakery, which was built of stone in 1867. A new bakery, built of stone in 1870, could furnish four hundred rations of bread per day. A single-story frame building on the east side of the parade ground contained the adjutant's office, including the library, and post chapel.

Surgeon M.M. Shearer described the stables in 1870 as "conveniently located, fitted with new stalls, gravelly floors, raised walk through the center, and dormitory windows on each side." A trash dump was situated away from the post, and refuse was hauled there daily by wagons.

Although construction continued for several years, the buildings erected were mostly temporary because Fort Wallace, like other frontier military posts, was expected to be occupied for only a few years. Because of the materials and methods of construction, partly done by troops without requisite building skills, the buildings required constant maintenance and repairs.

6

The Military Reservation

When the permanent location of a frontier military post was selected, a military reservation was authorized to prevent citizens from settling near the fort, thereby preserving the grass, water, stone, and firewood resources. A reservation, once approved by the Department of War and the Department of the Interior, reserved public land from settlement until a post was abandoned or, in some cases, special permission was granted for entry on a portion of the reservation. Such permission was granted on the Fort Wallace reservation when the railroad crossed a portion of the reserve and the town of Wallace was established as a railroad station on the reservation. These easements were confirmed by legislation after the post and reservation were abandoned.

The Fort Wallace reservation, with the post in the center, was two miles north to south and seven miles east to west, including fourteen square miles, just over 8,900 acres. The reservation was designed to include several miles of the river, the garrison's major source of water. Soon after the permanent location of the post was selected, an eighty-foot well was dug in an attempt to find a reliable source of groundwater, but a layer of shale containing petroleum rendered the water unsuitable for humans or livestock. The well was filled with stone rubble from the quarry. A dam was constructed on the river to capture surface water and provide ice to cut and store during the winter months.

The Fort Wallace reservation was surveyed in the summer of 1867 by H. W. Greenwood, a civil engineer working for the Union Pacific Railway,

39

Fort Wallace Reserve

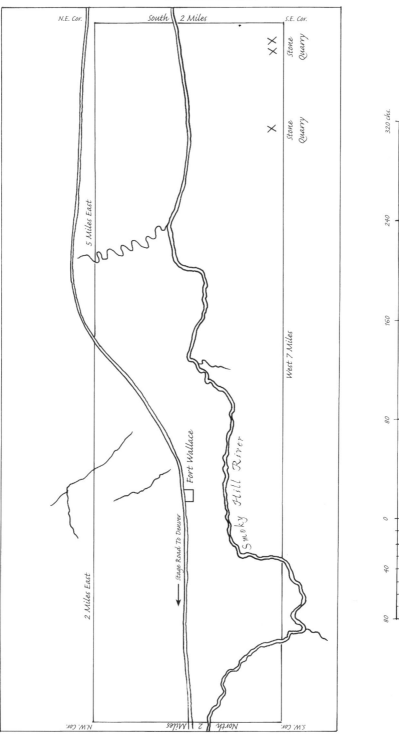

Eastern Division (after 1869 the Kansas Pacific Railway), which was building along the Smoky Hill route. The official designation of the reserve, including a detailed description of the boundary, was proclaimed by department headquarters more than a year later in August 1868. Except for the easements for the railroad and the town of Wallace, the reserve remained intact until abandoned in 1888 when the land was transferred to the General Land Office, Department of the Interior, to be opened for settlement.

Settlement near the military reservation existed at the time it was surveyed, and additional settlement occurred just off the reservation while the post was active. Soon after Fort Wallace was established, civilian settlement grew around Pond Creek Station, which in 1868 became Pond City and the county seat of newly organized Wallace County. The county was dissolved a few years later, however, because of insufficient population but was reestablished in 1888.

No organized county existed during the fort's early years, but the area that became Wallace County was attached to Trego County for administrative purposes. Settlers soon followed the soldiers to provide services, food, and other supplies for the post garrison, provide a civilian labor force for the fort and transportation firms, hunt buffalo and other native animals, investigate the possibilities for agriculture in the area, and locate possible town sites to be developed when railroad construction reached that point.

With the promise of the railroad and sufficient population, including the garrison of the post, Wallace County was organized in 1868, with the town of Pond City (formerly Pond Creek Station) as the county seat. When the railroad arrived the seat of county government was moved to the town of Wallace near the northwest corner of the military reservation. The anticipated development of Wallace County stalled when railroad construction halted temporarily at the town of Sheridan, fifteen miles east in present Logan County.

The arrival of the railroad at Wallace more than a year later did not immediately spur settlement of the county. Publicity about the land was not all positive. A correspondent for a Missouri newspaper visited Fort Wallace in May 1870 and noted that the railroad offered opportunity, but his description of the area did little to encourage settlement: "The great beauty of Fort Wallace is its unattractiveness, being surrounded by a desolate country, over which not a spear of grass four inches high, dare show its head for fear of the wild winds." In fact, by 1875 the civilian population was deemed insufficient to qualify for a county government, and the county was dissolved. The 1880 census, including the post garrison, reported only 686 inhabitants. Fort Wallace was abandoned in 1882, and within a few years railroad promotion of settlement resulted in sufficient population to reorganize Wallace County in 1888, with a population of 2,357. The county seat was Sharon Springs, several miles west of Wallace and the old fort.

7

Frontier Defense: Indian Warfare, 1865–1867

Fort Wallace was part of a network founded to protect commerce and travel along the Smoky Hill route, guard the mails, protect settlers who might come to the area, safeguard the construction of a railroad being planned to follow the trail, and find and punish Indians who committed hostile acts in the region. When possible, troops coordinated actions, such as escorting the mails or campaigning against Indians, with those at other posts. Supplies for the garrisons along the Smoky Hill Trail were transported from the Missouri River to Fort Riley, where they were forwarded.

Fort Wallace's soldiers found themselves in the midst of a vast region dominated by Indians, resisting the intrusions into their lands. Troops at Fort Wallace, including the garrison and units sent in from other points during times of crisis, faced more Indian opposition and fought in more encounters than those at any other Kansas military post. Most of these engagements were small, however, and few were consequential in the outcome of Indian-white relations on the Plains.

Troops were able, for the most part, to supress Indian resistance and keep the Smoky Hill route open. The completion of the railroad and the settlement it made possible, along with the destruction of the great buffalo herds on which Indians depended, sealed the doom of Plains Indians. Throughout the struggle for control of the region the army was constantly hampered by a shortage of manpower.

During the first years at Fort Wallace, when construction required much time from the troops, they also had to deal with Indians. The con-

Artist's depiction of Indians destroying tracks of the Union Pacific, Eastern Division, May 1867.

tinued raids on BOD stations placed Butterfield's business in jeopardy. The number of troops stationed at the new posts proved inadequate to safeguard the line. The heavy losses of equipment, livestock, supplies, and employees resulted in financial losses that forced Butterfield to close his operation. In March 1866 he sold the BOD to Ben Holladay, who operated a competing stage line to Denver over the Platte route.

Holladay continued stage service on the Smoky Hill Trail from the railroad, building westward across Kansas to Denver. He also suffered heavy losses to Indians and sold his entire business to Wells Fargo and Company in November 1866. On February 1, 1867, Wells Fargo, after suffering heavy property losses to Indians, sold the Smoky Hill business to the United States Express Company. Indian problems and losses continued, but the stage service operated until the trail was superseded by the railroad which also faced Indian resistance.

The commanders at Fort Wallace found it difficult to deal with Indians both in combat and negotiations. On August 25, 1866, Cheyenne war leader Spotted Horse and twenty-four of his followers came to the post to talk. Spotted Horse and two men were taken inside to meet with Post Commander Alfred Bates. The Indians proclaimed they were peaceful and intended to remain that way. They hoped the army would treat them as friendly.

The next day, however, the same Cheyennes went to Goose Creek Station, forced the agent to feed them, took all the provisions, and proceeded west to the next station where they stole the supplies. Spotted Horse then declared they would never surrender their homeland, and they would burn all the stage stations and kill all the white people along the Smoky Hill route unless Fort Wallace and the stations were abandoned within fifteen days.

Lieutenant Bates sent William Comstock, the post's chief scout, to investigate these warnings. Cheyennes informed Comstock their soldier societies had vowed that the Smoky Hill Trail would be abandoned or they would fight to close it. Clearly more trouble was ahead.

On September 19, 1866, an estimated 150 Indians, believed to be led by Spotted Horse, stole fourteen horses and two mules from the post while attempting to drive off the cavalry horses. A detachment of the Second Cavalry was sent in pursuit, but after about eleven miles they lost the trail in an early-season snowstorm. On October 12 Cheyennes burned Chalk Bluff Station and killed two employees. It was not possible for the garrison at Fort Wallace to protect all the stations along such a lengthy segment of the trail.

The Cheyennes were divided over the decision to close the Smoky Hill route. A conference with representatives of Cheyenne and Arapaho tribes and two special agents for the Bureau of Indian Affairs (W. R. Irwin and Charles Bogy) was held in October 1866 at Fort Zarah on the Santa Fe Trail east of present Great Bend. Cheyenne Dog Soldiers declared the terms of the treaties of the Little Arkansas signed the previous year unacceptable. They forced the peace chiefs, including Black Kettle and Little Robe, to refuse to accept amendments to those treaties, particularly a provision that their reservations would be entirely outside the state of Kansas.

The Cheyennes at the council obtained whiskey from traders and became threatening. Some of the warriors declared they would never surrender the Smoky Hill country. William Bent's half-Cheyenne son Charles urged militant resistance to the trail and to the railroad. William Bent was present with the annuity goods for the tribes, which he had contracted to supply. Because of his son's behavior and the threatening attitude of the Dog Soldiers, William Bent concluded that an agreement was impossible. He left the council. No agreement was reached. The Cheyennes returned to raiding along the Smoky Hill Trail.

Cheyennes attacking a working party on the Union Pacific, Eastern Division, August 4, 1867, from Harper's Weekly, *September 7, 1867.*

At the beginning of November 1866 Fort Wallace's garrison of sixty-three officers and men was inadequate to such a task. Post Commander Joseph Hale reported to department headquarters that the stage stations could not be defended properly with only the one or two soldiers he could provide each. He suggested that such protection was so inadequate that it was more likely to encourage rather than deter Indian attacks. Clearly more troops were needed, and reinforcements were sent quickly.

The garrison was increased later the same month when Company I, Seventh Cavalry, under command of Captain Miles W. Keogh, who also became post commander, and Company D, Nineteenth Infantry, joined Company E, Third Infantry, making a total of 195 officers and men. These troops were "now deemed necessary for the protection of the Stage line," and some soldiers were placed at stage stations. At the end of November 1866, for example, forty-five men were on detached service for one month to protect the stations at Cheyenne Wells, Big Springs, and Willow Creek.

In November 1866 Cheyenne Indian Agent Edward W. Wynkoop persuaded Black Kettle and Little Robe, while the soldier societies were away from camp raiding, to agree to the amendments to the treaties of the Little Arkansas. The peace chiefs, however, could not force the dissi-

dents in the societies to accept these terms or the original treaties. Wynkoop's efforts to obtain a peaceful settlement were frustrated by Major General Winfield Scott Hancock, commanding the Department of the Missouri, who ordered the Cheyennes to surrender those Indians who had raided along the Smoky Hill. Hancock declared that if the Cheyennes did not surrender the guilty parties, he would "attack them" with a large military force. He began making plans for a major expedition to defeat the Indians in western Kansas the following spring thus further expanding warfare.

During the winter of 1866–1867 military intelligence predicted increased Indian retaliation in the spring and summer of 1867. The tribal factions refused the terms of peace treaties and prepared to make a last-ditch effort to close the Smoky Hill Trail and stop the railroad from building through their heartland. In April 1867 Hancock launched his expedition to force the recalcitrant tribesmen onto reservations. Thus Fort Wallace, responsible for a large area in which strong Indian resistance was anticipated, received additional facilities and manpower.

In 1867 post construction was interrupted to pursue the primary mission of the garrison, control of Indians. Each mail coach was escorted, and small squads of troops were sent to protect some of the relay stations. On March 26, 1867, the cavalry company and twenty men from the infantry companies pursued a party of Cheyennes who had attacked Goose Creek Station twelve miles west of Fort Wallace. The raiders had time to disappear from the scene before troops arrived and were not found.

The soldiers' firepower was increased to match the expected increase in hostilities. At the end of March the infantry companies received breech-loading rifles delivered under an escort of a sergeant and twelve men from Fort Hays. Troops at Fort Wallace and those at several stage stations along the route east and west of the post received the new weapons.

In May 1867 Indian resistance increased as predicted. On May 1 Indians burned Goose Creek Station. They attempted to burn Chalk Bluff

Laying track on the Union Pacific, Eastern Division, west of Hays, Kansas, in 1867. Alexander Gardner photo no. 152. This photograph may have been taken by Dr. William A. Bell, who used it for an engraving for the frontispiece of his New Tracks in North America. *It is almost certain that Bell took some of the photos that are in Gardner's collection.*

Station on May 9 but were driven away. On the night of May 11 they tried without success to burn Pond Creek Station. The next morning the cavalry at Fort Wallace pursued that party but failed to locate it.

The same day, May 12, Indians stole the livestock at Willow Creek Station. On May 17 they stole the rations of the soldiers guarding Monument Station. During the night of May 26 Indians drove off a cattle herd at Pond Creek. The next day the cavalry recovered all but the five head that had been slaughtered by the Indians. This was the only instance during the month when the army enjoyed any retaliatory success.

A post officer reported that "during June 1867 two skirmishes with Indians occurred in this vicinity besides numerous conflicts at different points along the line of the stage road, resulting in the death of ten soldiers and many wounded." The post commander's monthly report listed many attacks on stage stations guarded by troops.

At Smoky Hill Springs, Indians endeavored to burn the station but were repulsed by the guard. At least two other attempts were made to

William Bent, 1809–1869, operated Bent's Old Fort on the Arkansas River near present La Junta, Colorado, 1833–1849. In 1853 he built Bent's New Fort, which was sold to the government in 1859 to become part of Fort Wise (later Fort Lyon). Bent served as Indian agent in 1859. He married a Cheyenne, Owl Woman, and upon her death married her sister, Yellow Woman. Some of his children, half Cheyenne, chose to live in Indian tradition. Charles and George were known to raid with other Cheyenne warriors. William Bent encouraged the government to build forts, such as Fort Wallace, to control hostile Indians.

burn the station and steal the livestock. Russell Springs was attacked four times, with the loss of two horses and one mule. Henshaw Station was hit three times, losing sixteen horses. Pond Creek was attacked three times and lost three horses.

Goose Creek was raided twice and lost seven mules. Big Timbers (also known as Blue Mound), located at a large cottonwood grove near the western border of Kansas, was attacked several times with one mule killed and three wounded. The livestock at Cheyenne Wells was raided during the night, but the attack was defended without loss of animals. All the stock at Hugo Wells was stolen. At Deering's Wells seven horses were stolen. Cedar Point lost seven horses. No troops were stationed at Hugo Wells or Cedar Point. All the livestock stolen from the stations was property of the U.S. Express Company. At least eight stagecoach drivers employed by the company refused to travel the route without a military escort.

Lieutenant James M. Bell, Company I, Seventh Cavalry, was sent from Fort Wallace to Denver in June to assess the situation and design a plan for the stage stations' defense. He stationed a few soldiers as guards at most of the stations along the way. He later recalled, with some exaggeration:

Captain Myles W. Keogh, Seventh Cavalry, commanded Fort Wallace from November 1866 to July 1867. A native of Ireland (born 1842), he served in the Union army during the Civil War. He was appointed captain of Company I, Seventh Cavalry, in 1866 and served in that office until his death at the Little Big Horn on June 25, 1876. His horse, Comanche, was considered to be the only U.S. military survivor at "Custer's last stand."

The Indians were so active and persistent that nearly all the stations were destroyed, horses stolen and keepers killed for a distance of 150 miles east and west of Wallace, so that it became necessary for a time to haul the stages over this part of the route with government mules. Two coaches were run together, one carrying the passengers and mail, the other an escort of soldiers.

Lieutenant Bell noted that the route was considered so dangerous that few passengers traveled on the coaches. The coach on which he returned to Fort Wallace from Denver was attacked on June 11, a few miles west of the Kansas border and Big Timbers Station. The soldiers on board shot several Indians and the raiding party dispersed. One of the soldiers on the coach, Private Jacob Miller, Third Infantry, was killed.

In addition to the stage line raids, Indians killed four citizens within eight miles of the post. A wagon train loaded with wool lost all sixty of its mules when Indians attacked it near Hugo. On June 15 the westbound coaches, with passengers and escort totaling twenty-three men, were attacked by an estimated two hundred to three hundred Indians. Two soldiers, Privates Edward McNally and Joseph Waldroff, Third Infantry, were

General Winfield Scott Hancock compiled an outstanding record during the Civil War, but he had little understanding of Indians when he became commander of the Department of the Missouri in 1866. His expedition against Plains Indians in 1867, known as Hancock's war, increased warfare on the Plains. Hancock visited Fort Wallace during the campaign, and part of his expeditionary force led by George A. Custer camped near the post. Hancock was replaced as department commander by General Philip H. Sheridan. Hancock was nominated for president by the Democrats in 1880 and was defeated by James A. Garfield.

killed, and Private Morehouse of the same company was wounded. One passenger was killed and two were wounded.

The coaches returned to Fort Wallace. The stages attempted to travel eastward from the post on June 21 but attacks forced their return. The coaches started toward the east again on June 23. That evening they came upon the camp of railroad surveyors, military escort, and other travelers, including English physician William A. Bell who recorded his trip in *New Tracks in North America*. Bell explained that the coaches' escort mistook the sentinels of Bell's camp for Indians and fired at them. The sentinels believed they were being attacked by Indians. "Not much was said about the mistake," Bell noted, "for both sides were a little ashamed of it." But vigilance was essential with Indians threatening all travelers in the region. Bell reported that they "dug rifle pits around our camp" and spent a long night on watch for Indians, wondering if each coyote howl was a coyote or an Indian. The next day they entered the safety of Fort Wallace, where they "found the little garrison quite worn out by the dangers and anxieties of the last few days."

Farther east the construction crews of the Union Pacific, Eastern Division, building along the Smoky Hill route, were constantly harassed

Indian attacks along the Smoky Hill Trail increased after General Hancock burned the village on Pawnee Fork in the spring of 1867. Theodore R. Davis portrayed an Indian assault on a stagecoach in this illustration entitled Here They Come, *which appeared in* Harper's New Monthly Magazine, *July 1867.*

This photograph of a stagecoach with its military escort was included in Alexander Gardner's collection of photographs taken along the Union Pacific Railway, Eastern Division, in 1867 (photo no. 148). It was labeled "U.S. Express

by Indians. During late May and most of June they virtually halted construction. At one point Indians captured the end-of-track construction camp and forced the workers to retreat. Neither the railroad nor the stage line was safe. Stage service was temporarily shut down until the army could clear the route of hostile Indians.

At Fort Wallace William Bell met A. R. Calhoun, a Civil War veteran and newspaper reporter who wrote an account for Bell's book about events at Fort Wallace during the previous two weeks. On June 16 Major General Winfield Scott Hancock, who had led a large expedition

---

Overland Stage, starting for Denver from Hays City, Kansas." Interestingly, an engraving based on this photograph was published in William A. Bell's New Tracks in North America (1869) with the label "Arrival of the Mails at Fort Wallace." There appears to be some controversy about who took the photograph as well as where it was taken. Both Gardner and Bell accompanied portions of the railroad survey from the end of track at Sheridan, Kansas, to the Pacific in 1867. Both were hired as photographers for the survey, with Gardner as chief photographer. Bell, a physician from England, confessed that he had no training in photography, but it was the only position open and he took it. He learned the basics of the art, however, from John Browne of Philadelphia. Gardner was one of the nation's finest photographers, who had done excellent work during the Civil War. Gardner's collection of photographs from that survey, now held by the Kansas State Historical Society, includes scenes along the route from St. Louis to a point just west of Hays City. Bell's photographs include scenes at Fort Wallace. If Gardner took this photograph, it was taken at Hays City (and Bell apparently appropriated it for his publication and incorrectly placed it at Fort Wallace). If, on the other hand, the photograph was taken at Fort Wallace, as Bell published it, then Bell would be the photographer (the date of the photograph would probably be September 24, 1867), and Gardner would have added it to his collection as his own. Actually, Bell submitted his negatives to Gardner at the conclusion of the expedition and requested photographic copies. Gardner refused to supply the prints, but Bell obtained them from William Jackson Palmer, head of the railroad. In October 1868 Bell wrote to Palmer that he never wanted his photographs in Gardner's hands. Considerable animosity existed between the two photographers by that time. Gardner's biographer declared that some of the photographs in Gardner's collection from the survey "were undoubtedly taken by Dr. Bell. . . . As official photographer for the expedition, Gardner was allowed to publish all the expedition photographs under his name." Although the photograph on the facing page is in the Gardner collection, and an engraving based on it is in Bell's book, the actual photographer and location remain an enigma.

Captain Albert Barnitz (born 1835), Seventh Cavalry, arrived at Fort Wallace while on escort duty with W.W. Wright's railroad survey expedition in the summer of 1867. While at Wallace, Barnitz was engaged in one of the most significant battles with Indians fought near the post. Barnitz had served with distinction in the Union army during the Civil War. He was shot in the right thigh in 1864 and spent many months recovering but was back in action during the final phases of the war. He was appointed captain in the Seventh Cavalry in 1866. Barnitz was wounded at the Battle of the Washita, November 27, 1868. He returned to limited duty the following year and retired in 1870 because of his injuries. He died in 1912.

against Plains Indians earlier in the year with inconclusive results, arrived at the post. Calhoun accompanied Hancock and wrote of their arrival, "in the bright sunlight Fort Wallace looked like a beautiful little village." Calhoun remained at the fort when Hancock left for Denver a few days later.

Hancock was escorted by Captain Keogh and forty troopers of his company of Seventh Cavalry. This absence plus the absences of those assigned to escort and guard duties along the Smoky Hill route left the garrison with fewer than fifty men available for duty. Whether so few could defend it from a direct assault was questionable. Certainly the reduced size of the garrison invited Indian attacks. The Indians focused attention on the post for several days, apparently hoping to drive the soldiers from the area.

On June 21 an estimated three hundred Indians appeared near the post, and a party of about twenty harried the quarry teams capturing six

Fort Wallace, June 26, 1867. This photograph by William A. Bell shows the post adjutant's office, with several officers in front. Captain Albert Barnitz, Seventh Cavalry, wrote to his wife, Jennie, stating that Bell" took a photograph of myself and the other officers at the post." Barnitz is seated in the center, and Lieutenant James M. Bell, Seventh Cavalry, is seated on the left. The others were not identified, but "other officers at the post" on that date included Lieutenant Joseph Hale, Third Infantry and post commander; Second Lieutenant D. Mortimer Lee, Thirty-seventh Infantry and post adjutant; Lieutenant Frederick H. Beecher, Third Infantry and post quartermaster; and Surgeon T. H. Turner. Based on other photographs of some of these men, conjecture is that the photo includes, left to right, Lee, Turner, Bell, Barnitz, Beecher, and Hale. This photo was taken the same day that Barnitz led forty-nine men against attacking Cheyennes.

mules and mortally wounding the civilian driver Pat McCarty. Lieutenant Bell and the few cavalrymen remaining at the post engaged the Indians for nearly two hours, part of the time in hand-to-hand combat. Sergeant William H. Dummell and Private Frederic A. Bacon were killed; Private John Haney was wounded. The civilian employees and a few infantrymen supported the cavalry, and the Indians finally withdrew with losses estimated at fifteen to twenty.

Captain Albert Barnitz's fight with Cheyennes near Fort Wallace, June 26, 18 *from* Harper's Weekly, *July 27, 1867.*

Calhoun had ridden out to witness the battle. "I found," he wrote,

a number of wounded men, and an irregular line of soldiers and civilians on foot; while the mounted men, under Lieutenant Bell, were in the advance, skirmishing with the Indians. On the left of the little line of battle, a body of some fifty Indians rushed forward just as Sergeant Dummell, with ten men, appeared over the hill from the fort. Shouting to his men, three of whom followed him, the gallant fellow plunged in amongst the Indians; and for a few minutes the yells of the savages, the rattle of "Spencers," and the encouraging shout of the young sergeant, could be heard. Before assistance could reach them, the Indians were reinforced, and the devoted little band were trampled under the feet of the Indian horses. After the soldiers had fallen, the brutal Indians fired on them, and speared them. They were about scalping them, when the remainder of our little force rushed to the rescue, and the red-men fell back, carrying with them their own dead and wounded.

Calhoun believed that the Cheyenne raiders were led by George Bent, son of William Bent and his Cheyenne wife, Owl Woman.

Calhoun reported that "there was but little sleeping in Fort Wallace" that night. "Every man was needed, and there was an air of determination about the men which led me to believe that if the Indians assaulted the fort that night, their success would be purchased at a terrible price." The Indians did not return that night. The next day was "calm." Calhoun continued, "We buried the poor fellows that had been killed the day before in the little graveyard. . . . There was no rest, however, for the little garrison, nearly broken down with arduous guard and picket-duty. Every hour the horizon was closely scanned; not a tall tuft of grass moved in the distance, not an antelope bounded over the plain, that was not noticed by the sentinel."

On June 24 Captain Albert Barnitz and his Company G, Seventh Cavalry, arrived at the post escorting W.W. Wright's party of engineers, then engaged in surveying a railroad route to the Pacific. Calhoun exclaimed that "a thrill of pleasure ran through all" at the post to see the reinforcements. William Bell declared that a "second pleasure" came with the two coaches that arrived from the East with the mail a short time after Barnitz reached the post. On June 26 another large force of Indians came near the post. The estimated three hundred Cheyennes drove off four horses from Pond Creek Station then threatened the fort.

Captain Barnitz and thirty-nine men from his troop and ten from Troop I, Seventh Cavalry, "gave them battle" for more than three hours. The troopers were nearly trapped by the Indians following an attempted decoy and ambush that almost succeeded. The Indians, however, retreated with their dead and wounded.

Barnitz called it "a desperate little fight . . . doubtless the most extensive engagement that has occurred for some time, on these plains." Sergeant William Hamlin, Company I, Seventh Cavalry, was placed in arrest and sent from the field during the battle for cowardice. Hamlin

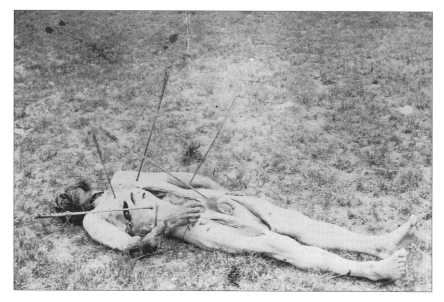

The remains of Sergeant Frederick Wyllyams, following the battle with Indians at Fort Wallace on June 26, 1867, was photographed by William A. Bell, who described the mutilation in detail in his book New Tracks in North America, *pages 62-65. Bell spelled the last name with only one "l." He wrote: "Sergeant Wylyams lay dead beside his horse; and as the fearful picture first met my gaze, I was horror-stricken. Horse and rider were stripped bare of trappings and clothes, while around them the trampled, blood-stained ground showed the desperation of the struggle.*

"I shall minutely describe this horrid sight, not for the sake of creating a sensation, but because it is characteristic of a mode of warfare . . . and because the mutilations have, as we shall presently see, most of them some meaning, apart from brutality and a desire to inspire fear.

"A portion of the sergeant's scalp lay near him, but the greater part was gone; through his head a rifle-ball had passed, and a blow from the tomahawk had laid his brain open above his left eye; the nose was slit up, and his throat was cut from ear to ear; seven arrows were standing in different parts of his naked body; the breast was laid open, so as to expose the heart; and the arm, that had doubtless done its work against the red-skins, was hacked to the bone; his legs, from the hip to the knee, lay open with horrible gashes, and from the knee to the foot they had cut the flesh with their knives. Thus mutilated, Wylyams lay beside the mangled horse. . . .

"So as I have said, almost all the different tribes on the plains had united their forces against us, and each of these tribes has a different sign by which it is known. . . .

"The muscles of the right arm, hacked to the bone, speak of the Cheyennes, or 'Cut arms'; the nose slit denotes the 'Smeller tribe,' or Arapahoes; and the

throat cut bears witness that the Sioux were also present. . . . The arrows also varied in make and colour, according to the tribe; and it was evident, from the number of different devices, that warriors from several tribes had each purposely left one in the dead man's body.

"I had made the acquaintance of poor Sergeant Wylyams only the day before. He was an Englishman, educated at Eton, and of good family, but while sowing his wild oats, he had made a fatal alliance in London, and gone to grief. Disowned by his family, he had emigrated to America, joined the army, and was daily expecting promotion out of the ranks.

"The day on which he was killed he had promised to help me in printing off some copies of the photographs which I had taken on the way. I had to print off my negatives alone, and to take a photograph of him, poor fellow, as he lay; a copy of which I sent to Washington, that the authorities should see for themselves how their soldiers were treated on the plains."

---

deserted a few weeks later. Indian losses were estimated at twenty. The troops lost one sergeant (Frederick Wyllyams), two corporals (James Douglass and James K. Ludlow), one trumpeter (Charles Clarke), and three privates (Nathan Trail, Frank Rahme, and James Welsh) killed, and two corporals and four privates wounded. The bodies of the slain soldiers were badly mutilated.

William Bell was sickened by the horrible scene. He described the mutilations in detail and photographed the remains of Sergeant Wyllyams. The gory details of the atrocities were published by the press, including *Harper's Weekly,* leading to increased public demands that Indians be beaten into submission as quickly as possible.

Warfare on the Plains continued. The garrison at Fort Wallace was especially vigilant and edgy. Barnitz, in a letter to his wife, explained. "Every night the command is turned out at least three or four times—the sentinels firing on wolves, or other objects which they mistake for Indians creeping up in the darkness." On July 1 a detachment of Seventh Cavalry briefly engaged a party of Indians near Goose Creek Station. On July 4 Captain Barnitz and thirty men escorted a wagon train from Goose Creek to Fort Wallace. This "lumber train," according to Barnitz, "consisted of 40 wagons, each drawn by about 20 oxen; the lumber, pine, is from Denver, and intended for completing the buildings of this post."

By July 1867 stagecoach travel on the Smoky Hill Trail was difficult, and impossible without escorts. General Hancock reported to his superior, General William T. Sherman, that Indians had attacked every stage station along the Smoky Hill for a distance that extended ninety-five

George A. Custer had little direct connection with Fort Wallace. He encamped near the post after leading several companies of the Seventh Cavalry on a futile pursuit of Indians during the summer of 1867. Custer abandoned his command at Fort Wallace and made a forced march to Fort Riley to see his wife, Elizabeth. For this and other infractions of military regulations, he was suspended from service, without pay, for a year. He returned to duty before the sentence was completed to lead his regiment in the winter campaign, 1868–1869. He defeated the Cheyennes at the Battle of the Washita in November 1868. His glorious reputation, earned during the Civil War, proved to be greater than his ability to fight Indians. He died with the officers and men of five companies of his regiment at the Little Big Horn on June 25, 1876.

miles east and seventy-five miles west of Fort Wallace. Indian attacks also were increasing along the Platte route to the north.

At Fort Wallace, Captain Keogh explained that an escort of six mounted soldiers plus additional troops inside each coach was necessary for safe passage. The post did not have enough manpower to provide such a detachment for every coach, especially because squads of soldiers from the garrison were guarding stage stations at Smoky Hill Springs, Russell Springs, Henshaw Creek, Pond Creek, Big Timbers, Cheyenne Wells, and Deering's Wells. Without the needed escorts, the stage line virtually was shut down. Raids on the stations and at Fort Wallace demonstrated the Indians' determination to close the route.

Indeed, the situation was perilous. The undermanned garrison was concentrating on protecting the post, which the Cheyennes could ostensibly besiege if they wished. The soldiers could provide little if any pro-

Custer leading the Seventh Cavalry in pursuit of Indians on the Plains during the summer of 1867. Sketch from Harper's Weekly, *August 3, 1867.*

tection to travelers on the trail. Supplies were diminishing, some of the food was spoiled, and it was not clear whether supply trains could make it through the Cheyenne barrier.

Even though the lumber train had arrived from Denver, post construction had come to a standstill because the soldiers were busy with military duties and the wagons were rarely able to venture to the stone quarry. Forage near the post was consumed, and animals could be grazed away from the post only with a squad to protect them. Morale at the post was low because of Indian threats, delay of the mails, and dwindling provisions. The soldiers felt isolated and wondered whether supplies and reinforcements would arrive in time to alleviate their situation.

Help was on the way. Because of the rise in Indian resistance, the garrison at Fort Wallace was increased from 243 at the end of June to 336 in July and 541 in August. More troops from Hancock's expedition, led by Lieutenant

Artist's depiction of Cheyennes and Sioux attacking a wagon train, Harper's Weekly, *August 17, 1867.*

Colonel George A. Custer, arrived in the region by a circuitous route. The enlarged show of force caused the Indians to back off, and the raids decreased. Small detachments from Fort Wallace continued to protect the stage stations until December. Freight wagons and stagecoaches moved again.

Custer's connection with Fort Wallace was important but brief. In preparation for the anticipated Indian uprising on the Plains in the spring of 1867, Department Commander Hancock had determined to take the offensive in an attempt to bring peace to the region. With a force of fourteen hundred troops, including eleven companies of the newly organized Seventh Cavalry under Lieutenant Colonel Custer, Hancock left Fort Riley in March. Hancock intended to lead his command along the Santa Fe Trail and deal with hostile or potentially hostile Indians, with force if necessary.

The expedition marched to Forts Harker, Zarah, and Larned. At the latter, Hancock planned to meet with tribal representatives to discuss the terms of treaties that some Indian leaders had signed. A spring snowstorm intervened, and when Indian leaders did not come to Fort Larned as expected, Hancock marched his command to an encampment of Cheyennes and Sioux on Pawnee Fork. Fearing attack, the Indians abandoned the village.

Hancock, who knew little about Indians and thought a show of force would cause them to submit to his authority, concluded that they must be hostile or they would not have fled. The abandoned village was appro-

priated, and Custer and the Seventh cavalrymen were dispatched to capture the fleeing Indians. Custer failed in that mission, and when he reached the Smoky Hill Trail he discovered that Indians had attacked some stage stations along that route.

When Hancock learned of this, he assumed the raids were committed by the same Indians who had fled the camp on Pawnee Fork. On April 19 he directed that the village, tipis, and other property be burned as punishment. The resulting conflagration was not confined to the captured village, however, for Indian resistance increased dramatically in response. Hancock's actions contributed to the warfare that had been expected, fulfilling the prediction. The Fort Wallace area was ablaze until reinforcements and Custer's Seventh Cavalry arrived.

After reaching the Smoky Hill Trail in April, Custer waited a month at Fort Hays for supplies. General Sherman, learning from Hancock that Indians were raiding along the Platte, ordered Custer from the Smoky Hill to the Platte. Custer led part of his regiment to Fort McPherson, Nebraska, and from there he was sent south to scout along the upper forks of the Republican River. Although Custer was expected to go to Fort Sedgwick, Colorado Territory, for supplies, he sent a company of his regiment to Fort Wallace to obtain supplies for his command. A detachment was sent to Fort Sedgwick with dispatches for General Sherman.

Meanwhile Custer's troops on the Republican fought a few minor engagements with Indians who eluded the troops and left them frustrated. From Fort Sedgwick came orders from Sherman for Custer to march to that post on the South Platte and contact Sherman for further orders. Custer did not leave the Republican, however, until the supplies arrived from Fort Wallace.

On June 26, the same day that Barnitz fought Cheyennes at Fort Wallace, Custer's supply train, which had left the post the previous day, was attacked by an estimated five hundred Cheyennes and Lakota Sioux. The moving fight lasted for several hours, with the Indians withdrawing as the train reached Beaver Creek. The supply train reached Custer's camp on June 28, and Custer began the move to the South Platte the next day. After more than a week's hard march, the command reached a stage station west of Fort Sedgwick.

Theodore R. Davis's portrayal of Custer's discovery of the remains of soldiers who died with Lieutenant Lyman S. Kidder at Beaver Creek on July 1, 1867.

Custer sent a telegram to Sherman who informed Custer that the Indians had transferred their raiding from the Platte to the Smoky Hill where he wanted the Seventh Cavalry to go. In fact, because Custer was tardy in reaching the Platte, Lieutenant Lyman S. Kidder, Second Cavalry, and ten men, with a Sioux guide, had been sent from Fort Sedgwick on June 29 to find Custer at his Republican River camp and deliver orders that directed Custer to move toward Fort Wallace in search of hostile Indians. Kidder's party hunted for Custer on the Republican and, not finding him, headed toward Fort Wallace. On the way, Kidder and his entire detachment were killed by a party of Indians on Beaver Creek on July 1, 1867.

Custer headed his troops, many of whom were disgruntled and some of whom soon deserted, toward Fort Wallace. At Beaver Creek they found and buried the mutilated remains of the Kidder party. Custer's command reached Fort Wallace on July 13 and camped about three miles west of the post. At Fort Wallace, Custer found the garrison hapless and weary. At about the same time, however, Indian resistance along the Smoky Hill diminished.

The only attack on the stage line in July was against a stagecoach near Goose Creek, but the escort from Fort Wallace "successfully repulsed" the Indians. An increase in the size of the garrison at Fort

Wallace and the arrival of the mails and supply trains, along with the cessation of hostilities, improved the outlook for troops at the post. The soldiers continued to escort the mails and guard the stage stations, but no major Indian opposition was encountered the remainder of the year. A volunteer battalion, the Eighteenth Kansas Cavalry, was raised to help guard railroad construction crews.

The presence of Custer's Seventh Cavalry may have contributed to the decrease in hostilities along the Smoky Hill. More likely, however, the Indians, who had been repulsed repeatedly by Fort Wallace troops, turned to other activities, such as hunting. General Sheridan made an inspection tour along the Smoky Hill route in early July and concluded that the Indian threat was not nearly so serious as citizens and the press had proclaimed. Military efforts were reduced after Congress established the Indian Peace Commission to attempt to negotiate a settlement with the Plains tribes.

The situation was quiet at Fort Wallace and Custer did not remain long. He had received no word from his wife, Elizabeth, whom he had left at Fort Hays several weeks before and whom he expected to be at Fort Wallace when he arrived.

On July 15 Custer and seventy-five men of his command made a forced march to Fort Hays, supposedly to obtain supplies for his command and the Fort Wallace garrison, but actually to find his wife. A detachment of his escort, unable to keep up with Custer's rapid pace, was attacked by Indians near Downer's Station and two troopers were killed.

Custer later claimed, too, that he was going to obtain medical aid for his troops because cholera had broken out in the camp near Fort Wallace. Interestingly, Custer left the camp near Fort Wallace on July 15 and the first case of cholera was reported there on July 22. It had appeared earlier at Fort Hays.

From Hays, Custer raced to Fort Harker by ambulance and from there to Fort Riley by railroad. He found Elizabeth safe and well. Custer was arrested, charged with abandoning his command without orders plus other misdeeds, and subsequently was tried by court-martial, found guilty, and suspended from command without pay for one year.

That year witnessed another peace treaty and another war on the Plains. Captain Barnitz, who returned to Fort Wallace soon after Custer left, was displeased that so little had been achieved. His observations to his wife, written July 28, 1867, were prophetic. "We will fool away the Summer here, without adequate force to accomplish anything, and next Summer we will repeat the experiences of this!"

8

Frontier Defense:
Peace and War, 1867–1869

The increase in Indian attacks in the spring and early summer of 1867 prompted Congress to establish the Indian Peace Commission to find a way to bring peace to the Great Plains. General Hancock's expedition had not only failed to settle the Indian problem, but may have exacerbated it. The peace commission decided that warfare was unavoidable so long as Indians occupied lands that U.S. citizens wanted. The solution, they concluded, was to settle the Indians on reservations away from the routes of travel and white settlements. The results were the Medicine Lodge treaties of October 1867.

The treaties, signed by some chiefs of the Arapaho, Cheyenne, Comanche, Kiowa, and Plains Apache tribes, provided that all warfare would stop immediately, any offenders against Indians or whites would be punished, and reservations would be provided for each tribe in present Oklahoma. The Indians agreed to withdraw their opposition to wagon roads, railroads, and military posts, to give up all claims to land between the Arkansas and Platte Rivers, and to hunt only south of the Arkansas River.

It looked good on paper, but some tribesmen and their leaders, who were not signatories to these treaties, refused to abide by the terms. They were not ready to give up their traditional way of life. They were determined to fight to protect their lands from further encroachment and the buffalo herds threatened by white hide hunters. The peace treaties did not bring peace, and the Indian war was renewed in 1868 as Barnitz had predicted.

General Philip H. Sheridan, hero of the Civil War, replaced Hancock as department commander in late 1867. The following year he organized Forsyth's Scouts, defeated at Beecher Island, and planned the winter campaign that helped force Plains tribes to reservations in present Oklahoma. Sheridan was general-in-chief of the army from 1883 until his death in 1888.

The army had no illusions that the treaties would be successful. General Sherman declared that negotiations with the peace chiefs was "senseless twaddle" and did nothing to deal with Indians who refused to talk and preferred war. Military leaders hoped the agreements would make their job easier because Indians not on the reservation could now be treated as hostile and dealt with accordingly. On the other hand, the problem of finding the Indians persisted. Major General Philip H. Sheridan, who had replaced Hancock as department commander in August 1867, had some ideas about how to deal with that problem.

The Medicine Lodge treaties were not ratified by the government until August 1868. The Indians had not moved to the assigned reservations. In the spring of that year, as in the past, many Cheyennes and other tribes in Kansas hunted buffalo and tried to continue their traditional life. They did not intend to surrender their land. The stage was set for violence. In the spring of 1868 some of the more dissatisfied Indians began to raid stage stations, assault railroad construction crews, attack homesteads, and steal livestock. General Sheridan argued that the solution to Indian warfare on the Plains was to defeat the hostiles and force them onto the reservations to stay.

William Comstock and his companion Abner Sharp Grover being pursued by Indians. From George A. Custer, My Life on the Plains.

Sheridan was authorized to initiate two plans for dealing with the Indians. A company of civilian scouts, led by Major George A. Forsyth, might succeed in locating the mobile enemy that often eluded military details during the summer months. More important, as had been demonstrated elsewhere, a campaign against the Indians' winter camps where they would be easier to find and their escape would be more difficult than during the summer months, might deliver the final blow to Indian resistance and force them to accept the reservations.

Before those plans could be implemented, Indian raids on the Plains and along the Smoky Hill again became threatening. In May 1868 several attacks were made along the railroad east of Fort Wallace. Indians burned several cars of a construction train, tore down telegraph poles, and raided a construction camp. The hay contractor for Fort Wallace, D. P. Powers, lost sixteen mules to Indians.

Few mentions of Indian problems in the Fort Wallace area appeared in 1868 until August. Meanwhile General Sheridan had traveled the Smoky Hill route, visited Fort Wallace, and laid plans for dealing with hostiles. These plans were taking shape when Indian resistance increased.

William Comstock was employed as an interpreter, guide, and chief scout at Fort Wallace, 1866–1868. He also operated the nearby Rose Creek Ranch where much of the hay for the fort was harvested. Comstock was killed by Cheyennes in August 1868. A few months before his death he had killed a civilian contractor at Fort Wallace who had refused to pay a debt and boasted that he had ridden with William C. Quantrill during the Civil War. At his trial in Hays City, Comstock pled guilty. Judge M.S. Joyce is supposed to have responded, "Ye are a damned fool for tellin' it. I discharge ye for want of ividence."

Before Forsyth's company of civilian scouts was organized and the winter campaign was implemented, Sheridan selected Fort Wallace's quartermaster Lieutenant Frederick H. Beecher, a Civil War veteran and nephew of the famous preacher and abolitionist, Henry Ward Beecher, to take three veteran scouts and guides to find and possibly negotiate with those Indians who had refused to leave Kansas for their reservations. Cephas W. (Dick) Parr, William Comstock, and Abner Sharp Grover were to attempt to explain government Indian policy to the Indians and try to persuade those who did not want war to return to the reservations. If the peaceful Indians could be separated from the hostiles, it would make the army's task easier.

Parr was sent along the Saline and Solomon Rivers east of Fort Wallace. Comstock, who had served as a scout at Fort Wallace since 1866, and Grover were sent to visit Indian camps north and west of Fort Wallace. About August 16 they were at the camp of Cheyenne Chief Turkey Leg, located near the headwaters of the Solomon River. Comstock and Grover were treated well until news arrived of fighting

Indian attack on a wagon train, Harper's Weekly, *September 19, 1868.*

on the Saline River. The two scouts were then ordered to leave for their own safety.

According to Indian recollections, the two scouts were attacked by a party of returning warriors. Grover, however, stated that he and Comstock were escorted from the Indian camp by seven young Cheyennes. As they rode away the young men dropped behind and, without warning, shot them from the rear. Comstock was killed and Grover, badly wounded, held off the Indians until it was dark when he escaped. He reached the railroad and, on August 18, Fort Wallace.

Comstock's remains were recovered by a detachment of soldiers and buried in the Fort Wallace cemetery. He had been an excellent scout for the army. He was reportedly the first owner of the Rose Creek Ranch, some eight miles west of the post, which contained fine meadows and was a major source of hay for the fort. Grover, incidentally, replaced Comstock as scout at Fort Wallace, and he was reported to be a later owner of the same ranch.

In August 1868 Cheyenne and Arapaho warriors launched a series of raids through the Saline and Solomon valleys of central and western Kansas, and hostilities were renewed near Fort Wallace. On August 19 at

71

Indians attacking a wagon train near Sheridan, Kansas. No date is given for the sketch, but the attack occurred in 1868.

Twin Butte Creek (also called Plum Creek) not far from Fort Wallace, three woodcutters were killed and twenty-five head of livestock were stolen by Indians. On August 22 a portion of Company B, Fifth Infantry, commanded by Lieutenant Hugh Johnson, was attacked about ten miles from the fort. The Indians were driven away without casualties to either side.

On August 23 two citizens were killed and scalped on Pond Creek. That same day Indians chased a stagecoach four miles before breaking off the attack. On September 7 Indians drove sixty-five horses from a hay contractor's camp twelve miles north of Fort Wallace. Other stagecoaches were attacked not far from the post.

In late August Kansas Governor Samuel J. Crawford appealed to President Andrew Johnson for aid, reporting that thirty men, women, and children had been killed and wounded by Indians in western Kansas during the previous week. He begged that federal troops provide protection for settlers and drive the Indians "at once, from this state." The number of troops stationed in Kansas was insufficient for that task, but General Sheridan informed Crawford: "We will not cease our efforts until the perpetrators . . . are delivered up for punishment. It may take until the cold weather to catch them, but we will not cease until it is accomplished."

As noted, General Sheridan was laying plans to resolve the Indian problem in western Kansas. The renewed warfare spurred him to action. He launched his plan to employ a company of civilian scouts to assist the

Major George A. Forsyth, Ninth Cavalry, was chosen by General Philip H. Sheridan to organize and command a company of fifty scouts, known as Forsyth's Scouts, in the summer of 1868. These scouts were sent to Fort Wallace to help fight Indians. They were defeated at Beecher Island in September of that year. Forsyth received three wounds during that battle and nearly died. He recovered and served in the army until his retirement as lieutenant colonel of the Fourth Cavalry in 1890. He was awarded the brevet rank of brigadier general for "gallant conduct and meritorious service" at Beecher Island. He served as General Sheridan's military secretary, 1869–1873, and aide-de-camp, 1873–1878. He wrote two books, both published in 1900: The Story of the Soldier and Thrilling Days of Army Life. He died in 1915.

small number of troops. On August 24 Major Forsyth, given the rank of brevet colonel, was directed to "employ fifty (50) first-class hardy frontiersmen to be used as scouts against the hostile Indians, to be commanded by yourself." Forsyth could "enter into such articles of agreement with these men as will compel obedience." Lieutenant Frederick H. Beecher, Third Infantry, was Forsyth's subordinate officer. A surgeon, Dr. John H. Mooers, was attached to the unit. Mooers reportedly was delighted with the assignment, stating that he "always wanted to see a real, live, wild Indian." William H. H. McCall, a Civil War veteran who had received the rank of brevet brigadier general, served as sergeant. Sharp Grover, still recovering from his wounds, was named chief scout.

Because the army had no authority to enlist volunteers for such duty, scouts were enrolled as quartermaster employees. Many of the men furnished their own horses. The army supplied equipment and rations. Scouts were hastily enlisted at Forts Harker and Hays and sent to Fort Wallace, where they arrived on September 5.

Frederick Henry Beecher, 1841–1868, was a nephew of the famous clergyman Henry Ward Beecher. Frederick graduated from Bowdoin College, Brunswick, Maine, in 1862, and immediately joined the Sixteenth Maine Infantry. Beecher was appointed successively sergeant, second lieutenant, and first lieutenant. He was in the battles of the Army of the Potomac from Fredericksburg to Gettysburg. Beecher was wounded twice in battle. At Gettysburg a Confederate artillery shell shattered one of his knees. Because of his injuries, he was appointed second lieutenant of the Veteran Reserve Corps in 1864. He served as adjutant under General Eliphalet Whittlesey. Beecher was discharged in March 1865. He was awarded the rank of brevet captain for gallant conduct and meritorious service during the Civil War. In November 1865 he was appointed second lieutenant of the Third Infantry and promoted to first lieutenant in July 1866. He arrived at Fort Wallace in November 1866 and served as post quartermaster and commissary officer until March 1868. During that time he oversaw construction of buildings at the post. General Philip H. Sheridan selected Beecher to supervise three civilian scouts during the summer of 1868. They attempted to persuade Indians in western Kansas, who had refused to go to the reservations assigned the previous year by the Medicine Lodge treaties, to proceed to the reservations. This mission was not successful. Beecher was assigned to Major George A. Forsyth's scouts as second in command. Beecher was killed on September 17, 1868, during the battle on the Arikaree Fork of the Republican River. Forsyth's Scouts sought refuge on a small island, which was later named Beecher Island (the island, really a sandbar, was washed away by a flood in 1935), and the engagement was identified as the Battle of Beecher Island. Beecher was honored a short time later when a military encampment at present Wichita, Kansas, was named Camp Beecher.

A few days later it was learned that Indians had attacked a wagon train near the town of Sheridan, about fifteen miles east of the fort,

Dr. John H. Mooers served as surgeon for Forsyth's Scouts. He was from the East and looked forward to seeing "real, live, wild" Indians. During the first day of battle at Beecher Island, Mooers received a bullet in the head. He never regained consciousness and died three days later.

and killed two teamsters. Forsyth's Scouts, as they came to be known, were sent to investigate. They concluded that the attack had been committed by some twenty Indians and followed their trail to the Republican River.

On September 16, still on the Indians' trail, the scouts camped near the Arikaree Fork of the Republican in present eastern Colorado. The following morning they were attacked by a large force of Cheyennes and Sioux. The scouts took refuge on an island in the creek, dug rifle pits, and fought back. All the scouts' horses were soon killed or captured. Forsyth was severely wounded, eight of the scouts were badly wounded, and ten were slightly wounded. Lieutenant Beecher, Surgeon Mooers, and several of the scouts were mortally wounded. The site was later named Beecher Island to honor the young officer who died there.

Surrounded, the scouts' situation appeared hopeless. During the first night volunteers Jack Stilwell and Pierre Trudeau were sent on foot to try to break through Indian lines and go to Fort Wallace for help. The second night Allison J. Pliley and Chauncey B. Whitney departed on the same mission but were forced back by Indians. The following night Piley and Jack Donovan made another attempt which succeeded. However, the

Simpson Everett "Jack" Stilwell, 1849–1903, was only eighteen or nineteen when he joined Forsyth's Scouts at Fort Harker. He had scouted for the army at Fort Dodge the previous year and joined Forsyth, he said, to help rescue "the white women who were taken prisoners." Stilwell was one of the scouts who slipped away from Beecher Island to obtain help from Fort Wallace. He and Pierre Trudeau set out during the first night of the battle. They reportedly tied blankets around their feet and walked backward from the island so as not to leave tracks heading away. They hid during the day and traveled at night. On the second day out they were hiding in a dry buffalo wallow and could see Indians in the distance. Legend has it that a rattlesnake crawled close to them, and Stilwell spat tobacco juice in the snake's face to force it to retreat. The Indians did not see them. Part of the lore of the venture of Stilwell and Trudeau is that they spent one day hiding inside the carcass of a dead buffalo. Whether that is true or not, they arrived at Fort Wallace on the evening of September 22 after traveling five days. They accompanied troops back to their comrades at Beecher Island. Stilwell scouted for the Nineteenth Kansas Cavalry and Custer during the winter campaign, 1868–1869. He served off and on as an army scout until 1881. He later served as deputy U.S. marshal in Indian Territory and Oklahoma Territory. He died at Cody, Wyoming.

"The Scouts and the Rattlesnake," from Nelson A. Miles, Personal Recollections and Observations.

scouts at Beecher Island did not know whether the couriers had been killed or were on the way to Fort Wallace. The scouts ran out of rations and consumed some flesh from their dead horses. The Indians kept them pinned down for four days, and the scouts remained at the site for a total of nine days, unable to move the wounded.

Stilwell and Trudeau, the scouts sent out the first night, reached Fort Wallace on the evening of September 22. They had traveled at night and hidden during the day. Post Commander Henry C. Bankhead sent couriers to find Captain Louis M. Carpenter, who was scouting the Smoky Hill Trail west of Fort Wallace with Company H, Tenth Cavalry. (This regiment, as well as the Ninth Cavalry, comprised African American enlisted men known as "buffalo soldiers.") Carpenter, accompanied by experienced scout James J. Peate, was to proceed directly to relieve Forsyth. The messengers reached Carpenter the next day. Bankhead led 106 men (comprised of a company of Thirty-Eighth Infantry, a company of Tenth Cavalry, a detachment of Fifth Infantry, and several scouts) from Fort Wallace on the morning of September 23 to find Forsyth. In addition to Stilwell and Trudeau, Bankhead was guided by scouts Homer W. Wheeler and Richard Blake.

Allison J. Pliley was a member of Forsyth's Scouts in 1868. He had been a teamster on the Smoky Hill Trail, freighting supplies to Denver. He served in the Fifteenth Kansas Cavalry during the Civil War and was hired as a civilian scout for the Eighteenth Kansas Cavalry in 1867, which he accompanied into northwest Kansas. He was wounded during a fight with Cheyenne Dog Soldiers on Prairie Dog Creek on August 21, 1867. Pliley was one of those sent from Beecher Island for help. He later served as captain in the Nineteenth Kansas Cavalry during the winter campaign, 1868–1869.

John Joseph "Jack" Donovan was from Denver, Colorado, when he joined Forsyth's Scouts. During the third night at Beecher Island, Donovan and Allison J. Pliley volunteered to try to reach Fort Wallace for aid. They made it in four days, arriving after troops had already departed to relieve Forsyth's Scouts. While Pliley rode to the Republican River to seek help from troops encamped there, Donovan led four other men to search for Captains Carpenter or Bankhead, who were searching for Forsyth's Scouts, and take them to Beecher Island. They overtook Carpenter on September 25 and reached the island the same day. Donovan was thus the first of the scouts who had gone for help to return to the scene of the battle.

Sigmund Shlesinger, a Jewish immigrant from New York City, had traveled west to Kansas in 1867. He freighted supplies to the railroad construction crews on the Union Pacific, Eastern Division, which brought him to Sheridan, the end-of-track town fifteen miles east of Fort Wallace. There he worked at odd jobs but was unemployed in the summer of 1868. He was at Fort Hays when Forsyth was recruiting scouts and joined up. He was only seventeen at the time, the youngest of the scouts. Forsyth reportedly had reservations about enlisting someone so young, but a veteran scout, Cephas W. "Dick" Parr, vouched that Shlesinger could do the job. He did. Shlesinger later wrote an important account of the Beecher Island battle.

Donovan and Pliley, who left Beecher Island on the third night, arrived at Fort Wallace on September 23. They had reached a ranch on the Smoky Hill Trail and caught a stagecoach to the post. They arrived after Bankhead's rescue party had departed. Pliley set out to locate a detachment of soldiers from Fort Sedgwick, Colorado Territory, under command of Lieutenant Colonel Luther P. Bradley, encamped on the Republican River. He found Bradley's command on September 25. Bradley sent Major James S. Brisbin with two companies of Second Cavalry to rescue Forsyth and his besieged scouts. Brisbin joined Bankhead later the same day.

Meanwhile, Donovan set out from Fort Wallace with four other men to overtake Bankhead or Carpenter and lead them to the scouts. They found Carpenter on the morning of September 25, and Donovan and Peate led the Tenth cavalrymen to Forsyth's Scouts later the same day. Carpenter's supply train of thirteen wagons arrived a short time later, and the starving scouts soon ate their fill. Tents were set up to protect the wounded. Assistant Surgeon Jenkins A. Fitzgerald accompanied Carpen-

Captain Louis Henry Carpenter led the first troops to relieve Forsyth's Scouts at Beecher Island. He commanded Company H, Tenth Cavalry, the African American buffalo soldiers. They reached the island on September 25, nine days after the battle commenced. Carpenter was awarded the medal of honor for this action. On October 17 he led two companies of the Tenth against Indians on Beaver Creek, for which he was promoted to the rank of brevet colonel. Carpenter had served in the cavalry during the Civil War, at which time he became a friend of George Forsyth. Carpenter retired from the army in 1899.

ter and treated the wounded as best he could. He found it necessary to amputate one leg of Louis Farley, but Farley had suffered too much and died during the night.

Colonel Bankhead's troops, accompanied by Major Brisbin's command, arrived the next morning, bringing Assistant Surgeon Theophilus H. Turner, more food, medical supplies, and ambulances. The dead were buried on the island (the remains of some were later removed to the post cemetery), and the survivors arrived at Fort Wallace on September 29. The wounded recovered in the post hospital. Forsyth's command had lost five or six killed (one scout was not recovered and presumed dead) and fifteen wounded. Indian losses were nine killed, including Roman Nose, and an undetermined number wounded. Sheridan's experiment with civilian scouts had not brought the desired results.

Forsyth had been shot in both legs and required months to recover. Surgeon Fitzgerald, who wanted to amputate one of Forsyth's legs, later asserted that Forsyth would not have survived one more day without medical attention. Forsyth was later awarded the rank of brevet brigadier general for his conduct at Beecher Island. Lieutenant Beecher was honored on October 19, 1868, when a military camp at the mouth of the Little

Arkansas River, present Wichita, Kansas, was named Camp Beecher. The camp was abandoned a year later. Captain Carpenter was awarded the medal of honor for distinguished conduct during the Indian campaign and for the forced march to relieve Forsyth. Colonel Bankhead was breveted a brigadier general for the prompt relief of Forsyth's command.

While Forsyth's Scouts were besieged at Beecher Island, Indian raids along the Smoky Hill route continued. Captain George W. Graham and his Company I, Tenth Cavalry, were sent from Fort Wallace to guard the stage line from the end of track at Sheridan to Denver. On September 17 Captain Graham and his troops engaged an estimated one hundred Indians near Big Sandy Creek in eastern Colorado. Graham reported that eleven Indians were killed and fourteen wounded while his losses were one man wounded and ten horses killed or captured.

Graham was awarded the rank of brevet major for gallant and meritorious service during this battle. His later career was an unfortunate tale, one part of which had a Fort Wallace connection. Within a few years Graham was unable to overcome mental problems and an addiction to alcohol. He was found guilty of selling government horses. On August 16, 1870, he was cashiered from the army for wanton disregard of military discipline.

In July 1873 an army paymaster, accompanied by an escort from Fort Wallace, was robbed by two masked men while on the way to pay troops stationed near River Bend, Colorado. Shots were fired and one of the robbers, George Graham, was wounded. He was taken to a Denver hospital, from which he escaped. He was later arrested, tried, found guilty, and imprisoned in the Colorado penitentiary. He escaped but was captured and returned to complete his sentence. Following his release, he was employed to guard a mine in Colorado from claim jumpers. Graham was shot from ambush and killed near Rosetta, Colorado, on October 12, 1875.

Soon after the survivors of Forsyth's Scouts returned to Fort Wallace, a number of them enlisted in a similar unit, known as Pepoon's Scouts or sometimes Forsyth's Veteran Scouts. Lieutenant Silas Pepoon, formerly of Company L, Tenth Cavalry, had commanded a party of scouts that accompanied Captain Graham and participated in the battle at Big Sandy. Pepoon's Scouts originally included some men recruited to serve with Forsyth's Scouts but either arrived too late or were considered excess because Forsyth was authorized to enlist only fifty men.

Pepoon's Scouts, as noted, were with Captain Graham and had hurried to Beecher Island when they learned of the battle. After returning to Fort Wallace, Pepoon was authorized to enlist more scouts to make a total of fifty. They went to Fort Hays which this special unit left October

Reuben Waller was a private in Company H, Tenth Cavalry, in 1868, stationed at Fort Wallace. He and his company participated in the rescue of Forsyth's Scouts, the first to arrive at the scene of battle. He later wrote about this experience. His reminiscences are an important primary source on the service of black soldiers in the frontier army.

10 to help the army find and defeat hostile Indians. Pepoon's Scouts participated in the search for Indians conducted by the Fifth Cavalry, led by Major Eugene A. Carr, during the fall of 1868.

The advance forces of Carr's Fifth Cavalry and troopers of the Tenth Cavalry from Fort Wallace encountered Indians in the region before Major Carr arrived to command his regiment. On October 14 Major William B. Royall, commanding the Fifth in Carr's absence, and several companies of the regiment were attacked on Prairie Dog Creek by a party of Cheyenne Dog Soldiers led by Tall Bull. The Indians killed two soldiers

Major Eugene A. Carr, Fifth Cavalry, led troops of his regiment against Indians in the Fort Wallace vicinity in the autumn of 1868. Carr, who graduated from West Point in 1850 and served in the West before 1861, was awarded the rank of brevet brigadier general for his service in the Civil War. He participated in the winter campaign, 1868–1869, and commanded troops who defeated the Cheyenne Dog Soldiers under Chief Tall Bull at Summit Springs, Colorado, in July 1869. He led troops against the Sioux on the Northern Plains in 1876 and 1877, and he fought against the Apaches in the Southwest, 1880–1881. He was promoted to brigadier general in the regular army in 1892 and retired in 1893.

and captured twenty-six horses. Royall sent troops to punish the Indians, but they could not be found. He then led his command back to the railroad at Buffalo Station between Forts Hays and Wallace.

On the same day Royall's camp was attacked, Major Carr left Fort Wallace, escorted by Captain Carpenter and two companies of Tenth Cavalry with Sharp Grover as guide, to join his troops in the field. On Beaver Creek on October 17 a large party of Indians attacked about 7:00 A.M., and they fought until 2:00 P.M., when the Indians withdrew. The troopers were fortunate to have seven-shot Spencer carbines, which they had recently received for testing. Even so, three soldiers were wounded and two horses killed. Indian losses were reported as nine killed, three captured, an undetermined number wounded, and four horses killed. Captain Carpenter was later breveted a colonel for this battle.

Carr and his escort returned to Fort Wallace on October 21, and the general traveled by rail to join his regiment the following day at Buffalo Station. They set out to find the village of the Dog Soldiers who had recent-

Samuel J. Crawford, 1835–1913, had a distinguished record in the Civil War and was elected governor of Kansas in 1864 and 1866. He promoted railroads and settlement, and he was determined to clear Kansas of Indian resistance. In 1867 he authorized the Eighteenth Kansas Cavalry to help fight Indians in northwest Kansas. He resigned as governor on November 4, 1868, to assume command of the Nineteenth Kansas Cavalry, which participated in the winter campaign, 1868–1869. He authored the book Kansas in the Sixties.

ly raided along Prairie Dog and Beaver Creeks. On October 25 seven companies of Carr's Fifth Cavalry and Pepoon's Scouts attacked a large Indian encampment near Beaver Creek. Indian men fought furiously while women and children escaped with as much as they could carry. An estimated ten Indians were killed and perhaps seventy horses were destroyed. The soldiers captured the abandoned camp and considerable property, much of which was burned. During the night the Indians made good their escape. After several days of fruitless searching, the column went to Fort Wallace.

Colonel Bankhead had led 170 soldiers and five scouts, with two mountain howitzers, from the fort on October 25 to reinforce Carr. They never caught up with Carr and returned to the post on November 3.

After the engagement on Beaver Creek, the Fort Wallace region became quiet as Indians moved from the area. Carr believed that his troops had forced them to leave Kansas. Actually the large encampment had broken into small parties, and some continued to harass traffic along the Smoky Hill route.

Captain Carpenter commanded an expeditionary force of three companies (two of Tenth Cavalry and one of Thirty-Eighth Infantry) sent from Fort Wallace on November 20, 1868, to proceed "via Fort Aubry to Sand Creek on the Santa Fe Road, and from there via the Pawnee Fork and Walnut Creek to the Smoky Hill River and by that stream to return to Fort Wallace" to search for Indians. They returned to the post on December 8, having seen only one sign of Indians, a trail left by some eighty lodges at least a week earlier.

On December 20, 1868, Captain Edmond Butler, Fifth Infantry, led eighty-nine men of his regiment from Fort Wallace to exhume the remains of the men who had been buried at Beecher Island. These soldiers were accompanied by Surgeon Turner, a hospital steward, Sharp Grover, and four other scouts. They marched through snow and met Sioux Indians who offered no resistance. While the party was disinterring the bodies, more Indians closed in and briefly exchanged gunfire before retreating. As soon as the remains that could be found were recovered, Butler led his men quickly back to Fort Wallace. Indians had ransacked some of the graves, and the bodies of Beecher, Mooers, and William Wilson were never found. The remains of Louis Farley and George Culver were reburied in the post cemetery.

Sheridan's second plan, the winter campaign, was organized and carried out from other military posts, including Forts Hays and Dodge in Kansas, and Camp Supply in Indian Territory (present Oklahoma). Three columns of troops (one each from Fort Dodge in Kansas, Fort Lyon in Colorado Territory, and Fort Bascom in New Mexico Territory) were sent to attack the Indians' winter camps in November 1868.

Major Carr and his Fifth Cavalry left Fort Wallace for Fort Lyon to participate in the campaign. William F. "Buffalo Bill" Cody and James Butler "Wild Bill" Hickok scouted for Carr and were at Fort Wallace for a short time. Pepoon's Scouts went to Fort Hays and escorted General Sheridan to Fort Dodge then on to Camp Supply. Lieutenant Colonel Custer was released from his year of suspension and returned to lead his Seventh Cavalry regiment from Fort Dodge. Governor Crawford resigned from office and assumed command of the Nineteenth Kansas Cavalry, a volunteer unit that joined in the campaign.

The payoff for the army came on November 27 when Custer's troops attacked and destroyed Black Kettle's Cheyenne village on the Washita River in present Oklahoma. After the Washita battle, Pepoon's Scouts escorted a wagon train of commissary supplies to the camp of the Nineteenth Kansas Cavalry, which had been delayed by snow from reaching the battle and was out of provisions. The scouts served with the expedition until they returned to Fort Hays the following spring.

At the Washita, Black Kettle, an advocate for peace with the U.S. who had survived the Sand Creek Massacre four years earlier, was killed along

85

John Pope was commander of the Department of the Missouri when Fort Wallace was established in 1865. He was replaced in that office in 1866 but returned to command the department from 1870 to 1883. Thus he was department commander when Fort Wallace was closed in 1882. He had the distinction of issuing the order that established the post and the order that it be abandoned. A graduate of West Point in 1842, Pope had a long and distinguished military career and retired in 1886.

with many others. The fifty-three Cheyenne captives, mostly women and children, were taken to Fort Hays. Because most Indians accepted their reservation assignments after Washita, Indian occupation of western Kansas dwindled. General Sheridan was promoted to division commander in March 1869, and the Department of the Missouri was commanded by Major General John M. Schofield until April 1870 when General John Pope assumed that office. By that time the "Indian problem" in western Kansas was largely resolved.

Even after the Washita battle, however, Chief Tall Bull and some Cheyennes refused to go to the reservation. Early in 1869 Indian raids were reported at Fort Wallace. On January 8 Big Timbers Station was attacked, and Lake Station was attacked on January 9 with two civilians killed. Companies I and M, Tenth Cavalry, searched for the perpetrators along Beaver Creek and the Republican River but found none.

The scene around Fort Wallace was quiet again until April 16 when Indians drove a small detachment back to the post without loss to either side. On May 26, 1869, Indians hit a wagon train near Sheridan and wounded two teamsters and escaped with about three hundred mules. On May 31 Indians attacked a government supply train eight miles west of Fort Wallace. Two soldiers and five Indians were wounded.

In early June Cheyennes tore up the railroad track near Grinnell Station east of Fort Wallace and derailed a train. The passengers and crew, most of whom were armed, drove off the attackers. On June 19 Indians attacked a wagon train carrying military supplies west of Sheridan, capturing two mules. Company C, Fifth Infantry, from Fort Wallace pursued but failed to locate the perpetrators.

The same day a railroad survey party under protection of a detachment of Seventh Cavalry was attacked near Sheridan. Soldiers repelled the Indians, who counted four dead and twelve wounded. Two soldiers also were wounded. On June 26 Indians raided the town of Sheridan and killed one man. Attacks on the railroad and telegraph line continued, but these were protected by guards from the fort who usually repulsed hostile parties. Settlements in north-central Kansas suffered several attacks in which several citizens were killed and a few taken prisoner, including Maria Weichel and Suzanna Alderdice and her baby from the community of Denmark in Lincoln County. Suzanna was the wife of Thomas Alderdice and sister of Eli Ziegler, both of whom had served with Forsyth's Scouts and survived the Battle of Beecher Island.

The public was outraged, and the army was directed to end these hostilities. Major Carr led his Fifth Cavalry regiment from Fort McPherson, Nebraska, into the field again, accompanied by three companies of Pawnee Scouts organized and led by Frank North, with Buffalo Bill Cody as chief scout. They searched about a month before finding Cheyennes and Sioux. After a pursuit that lasted several days, Tall Bull's Cheyenne Dog Soldiers were defeated by Carr's command on July 11, 1869, at Summit Springs in Colorado. The Indians lost fifty-two killed, including Tall Bull, an undetermined number wounded, and seventeen captives. The two women captives were in the camp. Mrs. Alderdice, whose baby had died soon after she was captured, was killed in the battle. Mrs. Weichel was rescued, although she was wounded. The captured village, including eighty-four lodges and supplies, was looted and burned. Most surviving Indians eventually made their way to the reservation.

Thereafter, Indian conflicts in the Fort Wallace region involved bands of Indians who left the reservations and traveled through the vicinity. Meanwhile, the railroad was completed to the new town of Wallace, near the post, and into Colorado. Fort Wallace continued to protect the railroad with detachments of troops encamping at several railroad stations and to help protect the settlers the railroad brought to the area.

9

Frontier Defense: Peace at Last, 1870–1878

Indian resistance to the railroad, which had been strong before the winter campaign, continued when Indians were able to return to the area. On March 21, 1870, they attacked the guard at Eagle Tail Station, present Sharon Springs, Kansas. In May Indians killed a roadmaster and ten railroad workers between Lake Station and Kit Carson, Colorado. Company C, Seventh Cavalry, pursued but failed to find the perpetrators.

On May 31, 1870, Carlyle Station, present Oakley, Kansas, was attacked, with two soldiers and three Indians wounded. On June 3 Grinnell, Kansas, was attacked, and Indian losses were reported as three killed and twelve wounded while the soldiers suffered no casualties. Troops from Fort Wallace, aided by other soldiers sent into the field were involved in each of the attacks. Altogether, however, Indian resistance to the railroad was not serious, and the Kansas Pacific reached Denver on August 15, 1870, with the formal opening celebrated on September 1.

Indian resistance around Fort Wallace became sporadic. In 1871 only one incident was reported along the Smoky Hill route when a buffalo hunter's camp was burned and the stock taken. The perpetrators were unknown although it was believed to have been a party of Sioux from the north who had permission to hunt in western Kansas. No Indian raids were reported near Fort Wallace in 1872. During that year the post garrison was cut nearly in half, to an average of about 135 officers and men. No Indian depredations were listed for the state of Kansas in 1873.

"A Match Buffalo Hunt" from Tenting on the Plains. *Encouraged by military leaders, buffalo hunters eliminated the large herds in the Central and Southern Plains, removing the commissary on which Indians had depended for generations.*

It appeared that the forts along the Smoky Hill route had fulfilled their mission. Department and division commanders recommended that several posts, including Fort Wallace, be abandoned as they were no longer needed. Fort Harker was closed in 1873. Forts Wallace and Hays remained, however, to guard against additional Indian outbreaks. Some Indian raids occurred in southern Kansas in 1874 during the Red River War, which saw the final subjugation of Indians of the Southern Plains. In 1875 Cheyennes from the reservation were met by troops from Fort Wallace.

Meanwhile, buffalo hunters had eliminated the large herds in the Central and Southern Plains, removing the commissary on which Indians had depended for generations. This was encouraged by military leaders and made the Indians' return less likely. General Philip Sheridan testified before the Texas legislature in 1875 that the buffalo hunters "have done more in the last two years, and will do in the next year, more to settle the vexed Indian question than the entire regular army has done in the last thirty years." Only a few officers protested.

The army arranged a highly publicized buffalo hunt for Russia's Grand Duke Alexis in January 1872. The duke and his entourage were accompanied by officers Sheridan, Custer, and Forsyth, with Buffalo Bill

General George A. Custer (left) poses with Russia's Grand Duke Alexis during the highly publicized 1872 buffalo hunt.

Cody as guide. The hunting party traveled from Omaha to Denver and east toward Fort Wallace. The post supplied seventy-five cavalry horses and four ambulances, each drawn by six mules, to assist with the hunt. A large herd was found a few miles southeast of Kit Carson, Colorado Territory, and more than two hundred buffalo were killed.

Other hunting expeditions came to the Fort Wallace area. A party of British army officers hunted there in 1873, guided by post trader Homer W. Wheeler. Nearly one hundred thousand buffalo hides were shipped from Wallace during the winter of 1872–1873. In the next few years buffalo bones were gathered and shipped from Wallace by the carload. Soon the region's buffalo were eliminated. Many reservation Indians, who hoped to continue hunting the old way, were outraged and struck back, precipitating the Red River War.

Because Indians were raiding north into Kansas during the Red River War, troops at Fort Wallace were sent to scout through the region and, if possible, capture those found off the reservations. The garrison at the post also changed when the Sixth Cavalry companies were sent to join General Nelson A. Miles's column. These were replaced by Company K, Nineteenth Infantry. This company, undermanned and occupied with garrison duties, could provide little protection to the outlying area. They did recover and bury the remains of the German family in October 1874, victims of Indians who returned to the region during the Red River War.

John and Lydia German and their seven children left their native Georgia in 1870 for the West, first settling in southwest Missouri. Because of drought and ill health, they moved to southeast Kansas in 1873. The next year they decided to move to Colorado and set out on August 15, 1874, with their property in a covered wagon pulled by a team of oxen, with two cows, two calves, and a few chickens. They reached the Kansas Pacific Railway near Ellsworth and followed it to Ellis where they were advised to follow the old Smoky Hill stage route. They were informed that Indians had not raided along the route in more than two years.

They continued without difficulty for several days and on September 10 met two eastbound travelers who told them they should reach Fort Wallace the following day. They camped that night approximately twenty miles east of the fort. They rose early the next morning and started about sunrise so they could reach Wallace before dark. As they moved out a party of Cheyennes attacked.

The parents and three children were killed and scalped. The remaining four daughters, ages seventeen, twelve, seven, and five, were taken captive. The Cheyenne party, led by Medicine Water, included seventeen men and two women. They took the cattle, whatever they wanted from the wagon, and burned the rest. After traveling a short time they killed the cattle and roasted some meat to celebrate their good fortune.

They later rejoined Grey Beard's band of two hundred Cheyennes, some of whom had been raiding elsewhere. One party had attacked a Mr. Stowell and two boys who were gathering buffalo bones a few miles north of Buffalo Station on the Kansas Pacific Railway, killing one of the boys. The same party later killed buffalo hunter Charles W. Canfield, who had homesteaded near-by the previous year, on North Sappa Creek in Decatur County, Kansas.

Soon, however, this band of Cheyennes headed south out of Kansas, raiding along the way. They probably were the Indians who had attacked the settlement of Pierceville on September 15. Troops were sent by train from Fort Dodge to pursue them, but the Indians escaped and went to the Canadian River in Texas. There they abandoned the two younger German sisters, Julia and Adelaide. The older girls, Catherine and Sophia, were taken along.

Julia and Adelaide survived on the prairie for nearly three weeks before their captors returned to reclaim them on November 7, after learning that the army had demanded their release. The following day a detachment from General Miles's column, comprising ninety-eight men from Company D, Fifth Infantry, and Company D, Sixth Cavalry, led by Lieutenant Frank D. Baldwin, attacked Grey Beard's camp. After a five-hour fight the Indians abandoned their camp and escaped with their horses, heading toward the Llano Estacado (Staked Plains).

The soldiers killed one Indian who was trying to kill Julia. She hid under a buffalo robe and was found by the soldiers. Adelaide had been sent out for firewood and also was recovered. These girls were taken by ambulance to Camp Supply, then to Fort Dodge, and on to Fort Leavenworth, where they arrived December 1. There they were placed in the home of a post blacksmith Patrick Corney. Their grandfather, Thomas German, was informed of the tragedy.

The bodies of their slain parents and siblings were found by a hunter two weeks after the massacre. He rode to Sheridan and telegraphed Fort Wallace. Second Lieutenant Christian C. Hewitt led a detachment from the post to investigate. They took the remains to Monument Station where they were buried. In March 1876 the remains of the German family were disinterred and buried in the Fort Wallace cemetery.

The other two girls, Catherine and Sophia, were taken to the Cheyenne village of Stone Calf in New Mexico where both were adopted into families. General Miles learned from New Mexican teamsters that the German girls were at this village, and he demanded their release. In time the Cheyennes returned to their agency and surrendered. They were promised food and other provisions as a ransom for the captives. On February 26, 1875, Stone Calf released Catherine and Sophia German.

Sophia German

Kate German

Julia and Addie German. This photo was taken about six weeks after they were released by their Cheyenne captors.

They were taken to Darlington Agency on March 1, where they were enrolled in the mission school. They were told about the rest of their family and wrote to their grandfathers in Georgia.

They were asked to identify the Indians who had killed their parents and brothers and sister but could recognize only five. It was believed the others had fled from the agency. The Cheyennes' punishment for their part in the Red River War involved the selection of seventy-five of their leaders to be sent to Fort Marion, Florida. Included in this number were four who were identified by the German sisters as participants in the attack on their family. The remainder of those who killed the German family were neither identified nor punished.

In June 1875 Catherine and Sophia German were sent to Fort Leavenworth where they were reunited with Julia and Adelaide. Although their grandfathers in Georgia wished to have the girls join them, the four sisters were kept at Fort Leavenworth and provided for by the army. Patrick Corney served as their guardian. They accompanied his family when they moved to a farm in northeast Kansas. Eventually, in 1879, Congress appropriated twenty-five hundred dollars compensation for each of the German girls. All four sisters received an education and each married. Although they never reached Fort Wallace, except for the remains of those killed, the German family massacre was a part of the post history.

An unidentified party, believed to be Indians, killed buffalo hunter Charles Brown in December 1874, apparently near Lake Creek between Fort Wallace and Fort Hays. The garrison at Fort Wallace was insufficient—only sixty-two in January—to provide troops for the field. A detachment of troops left Fort Hays to scout for the perpetrators early in 1875 but were caught in a blizzard, and some suffered frostbite. When the weather improved they found a small camp of Indians, captured four, and took them to Fort Wallace. A few weeks later these prisoners were transferred to the county jail in Junction City, Kansas, to await their return to the reservation or, for at least two of them, imprisonment in Florida.

Such incidents as the attack on the German family and the killing of buffalo hunters may have been a deterrent to settlement in the region. The Kansas Pacific Railway, which had received large land grants throughout the region including Wallace County, promoted settlement to dispose of the land and generate freight for the line. For several years the railroad sponsored agricultural experiments along the route from central Kansas to Denver. These included planting wheat, barley, and rye near

Wallace in 1870. Later the railroad funded planting trees along Pond Creek. Although these experiments were considered successful and the Indian threat to settlement in the region appeared to be about over, settlers were slow to move into Wallace County. Some soldiers who served at Fort Wallace later settled in the area. A few apparently acquired homesteads before their army service was completed. Even so, the county was dissolved because of inadequate population in 1875. Indians returned to the area that same year.

In April 1875 about sixty Cheyennes escaped from their reservation in present Oklahoma, headed north across Kansas, and split into smaller groups. Second Lieutenant Austin Henely and forty men of his Company H, Sixth Cavalry, were sent from Fort Lyon, Colorado, to Fort Wallace to intercept these Cheyennes. Accompanied by Second Lieutenant Hewitt, Nineteenth Infantry, Henely led his company from Fort Wallace in search of the Cheyennes on April 19. They were accompanied by Surgeon F. H. Atkins, scout Homer Wheeler, and a couple of teamsters. Rations and forage were transported in two six-mule army wagons.

They were aided in their search by buffalo hunters Henry Campbell, Charles Schroeder, and Samuel Scrack, whose camp had been looted by one party of Cheyennes led by Little Bull. With the hunters' help, Wheeler led the soldiers to Little Bull's camp on the North Fork (present Middle Fork) of Sappa Creek, where they attacked on April 23.

The Cheyennes, in a horseshoe bend of the stream, were attacked by troops with the advantages of surprise, excellent position, and superior firepower. The three-hour engagement was a virtual slaughter, with twenty-seven Indians killed, including twenty women and children, more than one hundred horses and mules killed or captured, twelve lodges captured, and most of the Indians' supplies destroyed. No troopers were wounded, but Theodore Papier and Robert Theims were killed, as were two horses. This was considered to be the last battle between U.S. troops and Southern Cheyennes. The first engagement between Cheyennes and U.S. soldiers had occurred in July 1857 at the Battle of Solomon Fork, about fifty-five miles from the Sappa Creek battle site.

Wheeler and Henely were rewarded for their victory. In October 1875 Wheeler was appointed a second lieutenant in the Fifth Cavalry. He eventually rose to colonel and retired in 1911. He later wrote two books, *The Frontier Trail* (1923) and *Buffalo Days* (1925), in which he recalled some of his experiences at Fort Wallace. Second Lieutenant Henely was promoted to first lieutenant the year after the battle at Sappa Creek. He and a fellow officer of the regiment, John A. Rucker, drowned in Arizona on a campaign against Apaches on July 11, 1878. His engagement with Cheyennes was the apex of his brief military career.

Although twenty-seven Cheyennes were killed at Sappa Creek, more than two hundred of their people escaped. Other small parties of Cheyennes periodically were reported in the region, but none were captured.

On October 24, 1875, a party of Indians was sighted near Grinnell. The commander at Fort Hays was notified, and he telegraphed Commander Henry A. Hambright, Nineteenth Infantry, at Fort Wallace, which was closer to Grinnell. Hambright sent Captain John M. Hamilton, Fifth Cavalry, with two other officers and twenty-three enlisted men to investigate on October 25. Two days later, about five miles south of the Smoky Hill River near Buffalo Station, they located a party of Arapahos who displayed a flag of truce and claimed to have permission from their agent to leave the reservation to hunt.

Captain Hamilton requested to see the pass and was told the man who had it was out hunting at the time. While seeking this man, the soldiers found more Arapahos concealed in a ravine, making a total of about fifty. Some soldiers feared they were being led into a trap. One sergeant, reportedly trying to restrain an Indian who appeared to be escaping on his horse, grabbed the horse's bridle and the Indian's rifle. The Arapaho broke free and, according to the soldiers, shot at the sergeant. A brief engagement followed.

Considering his men at a distinct disadvantage, without cover while the Indians were protected by the ravine, Captain Hamilton soon withdrew with five horses killed and one man injured. Private Philip Bernhart was erroneously reported killed in action. Indian losses were unknown. It was the last engagement of Fort Wallace troops with Indians. The detachment returned to Fort Wallace on November 5. Meanwhile, troops were dispatched from Fort Hays to pursue the Arapahos, without success.

The Arapahos returned to their reservation and complained to their agent that they had been harassed by the soldiers because the man with the hunting permit was not present. They claimed that a soldier and an Indian set out together to find the man with the pass, and the soldier grabbed the Indian's rifle. When the Indian refused to let it go, the soldier fired at the Indian. The soldiers then attacked the Indians, who returned the fire and caused the soldiers to withdraw.

An investigation followed, with the Indian Bureau and the army reaching different conclusions. No one was punished on either side, and the matter of responsibility was never officially determined. It remained

Lieutenant Colonel Charles R. Woods, Fifth Infantry, commanded Fort Wallace from May 1869 to January 1870 and during April and May 1870. Woods attended West Point, 1848–1852, and remained in the service until his retirement in 1874.

an example of the problems inherent in the division of authority over Indian affairs between two government departments.

After 1875 Fort Wallace troops had no further contact with hostile Indians. Even so, scouting parties occasionally were sent out to investigate reports of Indian activity at a railroad station or a homestead, but the most exciting incident that could be recorded at the post in October 1876 was Captain F. B. Dodge's horse dying of a broken neck.

After 1876 the post garrison averaged fewer than one hundred soldiers, and they had little to do beyond routine duties and maintenance. Troops occasionally were called out for other purposes. In July 1877 a detachment of fourteen troopers of Company E, Fourth Cavalry, under command of Captain Peter M. Boehm, traveled seventy-five miles in search of a cattle herd that had been lost while being driven to the Cheyenne reservation for the Indians' food supply. In September 1878 a detachment of twenty-four soldiers searched for a band of train robbers, without success.

The "last Indian raid" in Kansas occurred in September 1878 when some three hundred Northern Cheyennes, under Chiefs Dull Knife and Little Wolf, fled the reservation in Indian Territory (present Oklahoma)

Captain Louis T. Morris, Third Infantry, commanded Fort Wallace from May 1872 to January 1874.

Lieutenant Colonel James Van Voast, Sixteenth Infantry, commanded Fort Wallace several times from 1877 to 1880.

in an attempt to return to their homeland in Montana. They escaped several encounters with troops from other military posts, including an engagement with soldiers from Fort Dodge at Punished Woman's Fork (present Ladder Creek) north of present Scott City, Kansas, in which Colonel William H. Lewis, commanding officer of Fort Dodge, was killed. Troops from Fort Wallace were expected to capture the fleeing Cheyennes when they reached the Kansas Pacific Railway.

Colonel James Van Voast, commanding at Fort Wallace, placed squads from the post's Sixteenth Infantry along the railroad to watch for the Indians. He had a railroad train loaded with equipment and supplies, ready to roll east or west immediately when the Indians were sighted. The train was not needed, however, when the Cheyennes crossed the railroad undetected and proceeded northward, killing nineteen citizens in Decatur County to avenge the twenty-seven Cheyennes killed at Sappa Creek in 1875.

The Cheyennes proceeded into Nebraska where a dispute between Dull Knife and Little Wolf split the escapees into two groups. Dull Knife surrendered his followers at Camp Robinson, Nebraska, while Little Wolf led the remainder on to Montana. Dull Knife's band was held under guard at Camp Robinson until they could be returned to Indian Territory. When

Officers of the Third Infantry, 1870s. Most of these officers were not identified, but the three men seated on the couch are, left to right, Lieutenant Colonel John R. Brooke, Colonel DeLancey Floyd-Jones, and Major Henry L. Chipman. Floyd-Jones and Brooke served as commanding officers at Fort Wallace in the early 1870s. Several of the other officers in this photograph also served at Fort Wallace.

they refused, the army withheld food, water, and fuel. After suffering several days, the Indians broke out and fled the post on January 9, 1879. Soldiers pursued them through the snow and shot nearly half the Cheyennes. The survivors, including Dull Knife, were permitted to remain at Pine Ridge.

Little Wolf and his followers made it to Montana and surrendered to troops near Fort Keogh. Dull Knife's people joined them at Fort Keogh the following year. In 1884, the year after Dull Knife died, Northern Cheyennes were granted a permanent reservation on the Tongue River in Montana where the Lame Deer Agency was established. They had won the right to remain in their homeland.

After 1878 troops at Fort Wallace were engaged in routine garrison duty as the post was no longer required to protect the region. After December 1880 the garrison averaged less than forty, a caretaker unit to

These Northern Cheyenne chiefs, who were involved in the September 1878 raid in Kansas, are depicted here during their imprisonment at Dodge City, 1879. Top left to right: Frizzly Head, Wild Hog. Center left to right: Left Hand, interpretor George Reynolds, Crow, Procupine. Bottom left to right: Old Man, Blacksmith. Identification varies in other photos of this scene.

protect the buildings and reservation from settlers. Fort Wallace had served its mission well, protecting a vast region and engaging with hostile Indians on numerous occasions. Travel had been made safe, and settlers were able to occupy the lands from which Indians had been driven. As part of the network of Kansas forts established to protect overland routes, including the Smoky Hill Trail, Fort Wallace played a significant role in the military conquest of the Indians on the Central Plains.

10

Life at the Fort

The life of a frontier soldier occasionally was dangerous but almost always harsh and monotonous. Even so a supply of enlisted men was recruited voluntarily without the need for a draft during the post-Civil War era. Many men enlisted because they could find no other employment. Some were escaping the responsibilities of civilian life, a strict family, or a criminal past. A few may have viewed the army as a place for adventure or an opportunity to see the American West.

Many soldiers also were illiterate and joined the army because they were unable to qualify for other jobs. Many recent emigrants to the United States enlisted to have a job and, in some cases, learn the English language. Pay was low, even though food, shelter, clothing, medical care, soap, and candles were provided. Discipline was severe, which caused numerous soldiers to desert from the service before their five-year enlistment expired. Desertion was a problem that the army failed to solve until the frontier era was past.

Military pay was an important factor. Immediately after the Civil War privates entered the service with a salary of sixteen dollars per month. That was reduced in 1870 when a private received thirteen dollars per month during his first two years of service and, if he fulfilled his term of enlistment and joined up for another five years, he would receive eighteen dollars per month for five years, with an additional one dollar per month for each five-year period he served. Corporals received from fifteen to twenty dollars per month, depending on length of service, with an additional one dollar added during each additional five-year enlistment. The base pay for other noncommissioned officers was eighteen to twenty-three dollars for a duty sergeant, twenty-five to thirty dollars for a first sergeant.

A soldier's income paid the company laundress, company tailor, and barber, for personal items purchased at the post trader's store (tobacco, candy, toothbrush, comb, food, beer, and whiskey), for recreational activities outside the post, and, if any remained, to send home to the family or to save for a return to civilian life. Some soldiers did not consider the pay commensurate with the work and risks required and did not hesitate to desert to escape the severity of military discipline or to take advantage of another opportunity, such as going to the gold fields in Colorado.

Only single men were inducted into the service, but an enlisted man could marry while in the service with the permission of his commanding officer. Only a small portion of soldiers married, partly because of the scarcity of and competition for available women on the frontier and partly because their pay was insufficient to support a family. Most wives of enlisted men were employed as laundresses.

Laundresses were the only women the army recognized as having a reason to live at a military post, with laundresses' quarters provided and established pay scales set for officers and enlisted men who used their services. There were no provisions for officers' wives at a military post. They were officially considered to be camp followers. Officer housing was assigned by rank, regardless of marital status, and a single captain, for example, could force a lieutenant with a family from adequate accommodations into a single room or, if nothing else were available, a tent.

The daily-duty routine of the garrison, similar to that of every military post, was fixed by a schedule with changes announced by bugle calls. A typical schedule, established in August 1866, may serve as an example.

Reveille	Ten minutes before sunrise
Stable Call	Immediately after reveille
Sick Call	6:00 A.M.
Water Call	6:00 A.M.
Breakfast Call	6:30 A.M.
Fatigue Call	7:00 A.M.
Guard Mounting	8:00 A.M.
Duty Recall	12:00 M. [noon]
Dinner Call	12:00 M.
Fatigue Call	1:00 P.M.
Stable Call	5:30 P.M.
Retreat	Sunset
Tattoo	8:00 P.M.
Taps	8:30 P.M.

Supper was by company after other duties ended. If military drill were held, it was usually scheduled during the afternoon. On Sunday, inspection was at 8:00 A.M., with guard mounting immediately after inspection. When soldiers were not on call, they had free time, but could not leave the post without permission, and they were subject to call as needed.

Certain military ceremonies were regularly observed. The flag over the parade ground was raised each morning and lowered each evening with a proper salute from the troops, including bugle calls and the firing of a gun. A dress parade was held weekly, usually on Sunday. When a regimental band was stationed at the post, Sunday concerts were customary. The daily ritual occasionally was broken by the visit of a famous officer, such as the department commander.

Fort Wallace, as other frontier military posts, was isolated from settlements and sources of supplies until the railroad reached the area. Recreation opportunities were few on or off the post, although every military post, including Fort Wallace, attracted camp followers who offered whiskey, gambling, and prostitutes at establishments just off the military reservation.

The army constantly had problems with drunkenness among troops and officers. At many frontier posts more than 25 percent of the officers and enlisted men were alcoholics. Many more were given to periodic intoxication. Captain Barnitz declared that Major Wickliffe Cooper, Seventh Cavalry, committed suicide in June 1867 because "he had got out of whiskey!" The post surgeon's records were replete with cases related to excessive consumption of spirits. For example, Post Surgeon Turner reported in October 1868: "Several gunshot wounds one of which was instantly fatal occurred during the month, the results of drunken rows." Drunkenness was a frequent cause of a soldier's incarceration in the guardhouse, and it was a common component in charges preferred before a court-martial. It was a widespread complaint that little could be done at a military post for a few days after the paymaster paid the troops because of widespread intoxication and its unpleasant consequences. Not all soldiers were addicted, but many were.

In 1880 retired officer Duane M. Greene, who had served at posts in Kansas with the Third Infantry and Sixth Cavalry, wrote a book about the army. He noted that intoxication of officers and enlisted men was notorious. He declared that "the blighting curse of intemperance destroys ninety per cent more of the Army than powder and ball."

The major source of alcohol was the post trader's store. "Virtually," Green wrote, "the Army is a school of dissipation; and it really seems as if the establishment were kept up chiefly for the benefit of the Post Traders."

The Third Infantry Band was stationed at Fort Wallace from October 14, 1871, to May 10, 1872. This band gave a concert for the buffalo hunting party of Grand Duke Alexis in January 1872.

He declared of post traders, "their chief business is to sell intoxicating liquors to the troops." As a result, "they get rich in a short time—rich by destroying the bodies and souls of human beings,—and their occupation is dignified by the guarantee and protection of the Government!"

Green also observed that some soldiers joined the army because they were "inveterate drunkards" who were "unable to obtain employment at their trades." Even if they were not heavy drinkers when they joined, the pressures to consume were powerful.

> Young men not inclined to intemperate habits before entering the service soon acquire them after joining. . . . They are compelled to associate with uncongenial people. . . . On pay-day, they see that drunkenness is almost universal—seemingly an obligation—and, unwilling to shirk anything that pertains to duty, they join in the common revelry with a vigor that soon begets the title of "veteran." Such is the force of example when it is constantly before a man's eyes.

Even when post commanders attempted to restrict or prohibit access to alcohol, drunkenness remained a problem. Beer and whiskey usually were available for those who could afford the price, until President

Rutherford B. Hayes banned all hard liquor from military posts in 1881. At Fort Wallace the post trader usually charged from fifty cents to one dollar for a quart of beer, and whiskey was available for ten to twenty-five cents per drink or $1.50 for a quart bottle. The abuse of alcohol remained a prime problem in the enforcement of army discipline.

LIQUOR AT FORT WALLACE

General Orders, No. 4, July 18, 1866:

Hereafter the Sutler's Store will be closed to all enlisted men at retreat and no sales will be made to them except between the hours of 8 a.m. and retreat on week days and on Sundays the Store will be kept closed during the day.

Every enlisted man of the permanent garrison will be allowed to purchase three drinks of liquor per day for himself; he will in no case give, sell or otherwise dispose of the same to any other Soldier or Citizen.

With the above exception liquor will not be sold to either enlisted men or citizens except upon the approval of the commanding officer of the Post.

Any Soldier who shall be detected violating the provision of this order or in a state of intoxication shall have his name stricken from the list [of those who may purchase liquor] not to be replaced thereon for the period of three months.

General Orders No. 10, Sept. 24, 1866:

The post sutler will sell no more liquor to enlisted men until further orders from headquarters.

Military regulations were detailed and strict and provided for punishment by court-martial, including loss of pay and confinement in the post guardhouse, for a multitude of infractions, some serious and many trivial. The records of Fort Wallace, as well as those of every other military post, were filled with the proceedings of courts-martial. Such duty occupied much of the officers' time. It was a rare soldier who escaped an appearance in court during a five-year-term of service. The soldiers' morale was depressed by the heavy-handed system of military justice and by the nonmilitary work they were required to perform.

Although soldiers thought they had enlisted to carry a rifle, learn military tactics, and fight when necessary, most of them found that life at a military post primarily included guard duty, fatigue duty, kitchen police, and extra duty as laborers (erecting and maintaining buildings, quarrying stone, digging latrines, and loading and unloading supplies). A number of

Post trader's store, Fort Wallace, 1868. Homer W. Wheeler is second from the right.

soldiers complained that they spent more time with a pick and shovel than with a rifle, and they also complained about the ubiquitous guard duty. They usually welcomed any assignment, such as escort duty or an expedition to search for hostile Indians, which took them into the field and away from the labors of the garrison.

In or out of the garrison, they also complained about the food. The soldiers were provided a monotony of basic foods including, according to army regulations, hash, stew, soup, vegetables (usually dried or canned, sometimes fresh if a post garden were successful), beans, bread, hardtack (dubbed "cast-iron biscuits"), salt pork, fresh beef or mutton, coffee, tea, sugar, salt, vinegar, and molasses. All items, of course, were not available at all times. Soldiers spent a considerable portion of their pay for additional food at the trader's store, where canned goods and delicacies were typically available at a high price.

Because the commissary department procured some foodstuffs in distant markets and shipped them long distances, there were problems with deterioration and spoilage. The provisions were necessarily stored at the post for months, during which time rats, mice, and bugs usually entered the commissary storehouse. The beef cattle supplied at a military post for slaughter were frequently of poor quality, and the meat was notoriously tough. One cavalryman complained that a piece of roast beef

he had for supper was so tough that not a dog at the post could chew it. Buffalo meat was substituted for beef when it was available. Some soldiers preferred it to beef. At times soldiers caught fish in the Smoky Hill River, but these usually were small and constituted an insignificant part of the diet.

Hogs also were raised at the post by enlisted men and officers. This supplemented the food supply but created problems of odor and sanitation. The post commander found it necessary to issue the following order on February 24, 1870: "Hereafter Hogs will not be allowed to run at large around the Post. All hog pens must be removed at once to the east of the post at a point not nearer than those already established." The ineffectiveness of that decree undoubtedly precipitated a tougher order on August 16, 1870: "All hogs found running at large after 3 o'clock PM today will be shot."

Hogs were optional, but each frontier military post was required to plant a garden to provide fresh vegetables in season. At Fort Wallace these were seldom a success. In 1867 the post surgeon reported that the post garden "again failed as it had done the year before, the grasshoppers consuming what nature had allowed to grow." Of those insects, Lieutenant David W. Wallingford, Seventh Cavalry, reported to Governor Crawford on September 9, 1867: "The grasshoppers here might be measured by the cart load. The heavens are filled with them and the earth covered with them. In fact we have them to eat for dinner and supper. At breakfast they are too stiff to get into our food, for we have breakfast very early, so it is one meal that is not flavored with them."

Some fresh vegetables were raised by civilians near the post. In 1868, for example, two men were reported to have large gardens planted close to Pond Creek. They could not, however, fill the demands of the garrison. In 1870 post surgeon M.M. Shearer reported that "the failure of the post garden located here for three successive summers would seem to demonstrate the incapacity of the soil and climate or the want of practical agricultural knowledge on the part of the garrison."

In 1873 an enterprising citizen, George Allaman, settled south of Pond City, just west of the military reservation near the Smoky Hill River. He

Private L.G. Grant, Fifth Infantry, at Fort Wallace. Companies of the regiment were stationed at the post from August 1867 to October 1871, and this photograph most likely was taken during that time.

constructed a small dam and a mile-long irrigation ditch to produce "cabbages, potatoes, onions, and other garden stuff" to sell to the fort. Allaman's project, considered to be the first successful irrigation undertaking in western Kansas, continued beyond the life of the post. Allaman family descendants still occupied the same property at this writing in 1997.

In 1874 an attempt was made to irrigate the post garden. Post surgeon Francis H. Atkins noted in June that the "garden has yielded a considerable quantity of lettuce, radishes, onions, with some beets and peases—the onions alone not being of coarse and inferior quality." The following month he explained, "the post garden ceased to exist about July 1st the grasshoppers being in excess." Throughout its occupation Fort Wallace had a shortage of fresh vegetables.

Firewood was also in short supply at Fort Wallace. Few trees grew along the river and creeks because periodic prairie fires prevented their growth except in protected areas, and most trees located in the vicinity were soon harvested. A visitor at Fort Wallace in 1870 declared, "It is a

Private F. Wegener, Company B, Fifth Infantry, at Fort Wallace. Company B of the regiment was stationed at the post from August 1867 to October 1871, and this photograph probably was taken during that time.

day's journey to a tree." Wood was usually supplied by a civilian contractor, and the best source was the large cottonwood grove at Big Timber to the west. The woodcutters were protected from Indians by a guard detailed from the garrison.

Hay for livestock was also provided by contractors under similar conditions. Grass for hay was more readily available than firewood along the streams although the best hay meadows were about eight miles west of the fort at Rose Creek Ranch. As previously noted this ranch was originally owned by William Comstock. Other owners included Frank Dixon and Sharp Grover, both of whom, as had Comstock, met violent ends.

Homer W. Wheeler, who became a commissary clerk at Fort Wallace in 1868 and served as the post trader 1870-1875, also owned Rose Creek Ranch and furnished hay for the army. Hay was also harvested at other places within a few miles of the post. In 1873, for example, nine hundred tons of hay were furnished the post.

Hay, when harvested, was stacked near the post for use during winter months when grazing for livestock was not available. The beef herd for the commissary was provided by a contractor who grazed the herd near the post when possible. The cattle were slaughtered at the post as needed.

Food was essential to soldiers, and rest and relaxation were desirable. The army provided no recreational programs or facilities for troops during the era. The following holidays were observed by suspending all duties except for necessary policing of the post: New Year's Day, George Washington's Birthday, Independence Day, Thanksgiving, and Christmas.

Officers and their families constituted a society almost completely separated from the enlisted men although they did join in dances and musical entertainments. Musicals and plays, performed by enlisted men with occasional help from officers and their families, were sponsored by officers and their wives. In the evenings officers and their wives made formal calls, and officers frequently entertained their peers with supper and an evening playing cards or some other entertainment. Single officers usually were included in leisure activities.

Enlisted men occupied their free time with a variety of activities. In addition to the drinking, gambling, and whoring, soldiers fished and hunted, participated in sports (footraces, horse races, and baseball were popular), visited with their fellow soldiers (an eastern journalist who visited Fort Wallace in 1868 noted that off-duty time was generally passed in "prolonged conversations"), played musical instruments and sang, and read any mail received and books and periodicals from the post library. The library included more than two hundred volumes of history, biography, and literature, as well as several newspapers and magazines. Many soldiers were illiterate, but those who could read and write frequently read to and wrote for those who could not. A number of men also learned to read and write in the post school provided for them.

POST LIBRARY

General Orders No. 11, Mar. 26, 1869:

The following rules and regulations will be observed by persons obtaining Books from the Post Library,

1. But one book at a time will be allowed to be taken out by any one person.
2. Books will not be retained out over one week.
3. The money value of any book injured or lost will be charged to the person by whom it was taken out.
4. Officers or Enlisted men leaving the post for a period of over three days will return any books they may have out before leaving the Post.
5. The library will be open from 3 to 4 o'clock P.M. Sundays.

11

Medical Care and Sanitation

The health of the garrison was of major importance, and it was affected by the environment, food, sanitation, and medical care provided. The health and sanitation of a military post were the responsibility of the post surgeon, who also oversaw the post hospital and treated civilians as well as military personnel. Occasionally he was required to accompany troops to the field, especially if an engagement with Indians was likely. Other duties included periodically inspecting the soldiers' food, keeping records of sanitary inspections (including the water supply, condition of soldiers' barracks, kitchens, and latrines, and the disposal of waste), summarizing daily weather conditions, and describing the native flora and fauna of the area.

Surgeons, assisted by enlisted men who served as hospital stewards, were required to handle all types of injuries and diseases with only limited supplies of medications and instruments. Dangerous diseases included epidemic cholera, diphtheria, influenza, and consumption (tuberculosis). More frequent ailments were a myriad of fevers, dysentery, bronchitis, the common cold, boils, toothache, rheumatism, pneumonia, scurvy, constipation, diarrhea, and venereal diseases. Excessive consumption of alcohol affected health and provided patients for the post surgeon. Common injuries included broken bones, lacerations, contusions, gunshot wounds (mostly from accidents rather than battles), and, in season, sunstroke and frostbite. Some troops also suffered from exhaustion and mental anxiety; a few were declared insane and sent to

Post hospital at Fort Wallace, July 15, 1868. This hospital was destroyed by fire on March 12, 1872.

an army asylum. One post surgeon, Theophilus H. Turner, died at Fort Wallace, July 27, 1869, of "acute gastritis."

Medical supplies for Fort Wallace came from St. Louis, and typically a considerable amount of time elapsed between the requisition of medication or equipment and its arrival at the post. Ambulances and litters assisted in transporting patients from the field to the post hospital. Despite the limitations placed upon them by circumstances, post surgeons were mostly successful in keeping the garrison healthy.

The post hospital was an important part of the surgeon's facilities. At Fort Wallace the construction of the post hospital was delayed many times because it was not given a high priority by the quartermaster in charge of construction. He may have believed the hospital tent sufficient and that other buildings deserved priority. In 1868 the post surgeon complained that the hospital building, started the previous year, was not being completed. Work on the hospital came to a stop when many civilian laborers were discharged, but it was completed by 1870.

The hospital had a central building of stone, thirty-four by forty-four feet, with two wings for wards, each twenty-four by forty-eight feet with a capacity of twelve beds. Each ward had four windows on each side and one at each end. The central structure housed four rooms, including the surgeon's office, stewards' room, surgery, and storeroom. An eight-foot-wide hall ran through the center of the first floor, with stairs to the second floor which included quarters for the stewards, another storeroom, and a dead room for the deceased. Another building behind the hospital, twenty by forty feet, served as the kitchen, dining room, laundry, and cellar for the hospital.

The hospital was destroyed by fire on March 12, 1872. A wooden barracks was then converted into a hospital. The building was in poor condition, but it was partitioned into a ward, offices, and a storeroom. This building was moved (sawed into two sections and relocated beside the stone portion of the old hospital) and remodeled in 1874, when two wards were fabricated, ceilings raised, laundry and room for bathing added, and other improvements made to provide an adequate facility for the medical department. The stone portion of the old hospital, which had served briefly as the post chapel, was renovated for the hospital kitchen and mess room.

That same year the surgeon requested that a fence be constructed around the hospital "to prevent the cattle and hogs from prowling around leaving their filth and dirt, contaminating the water in the barrels and drinking it up, and occasionally breaking the glass out of the windows." He also noted that, during the previous winter, cattle had used the hospital building as a windbreak during stormy weather.

Whatever the conditions of the hospital, post surgeons were responsible for health care at the post. The post surgeon for the first garrison at Camp Pond Creek in 1865 was Acting Assistant Surgeon Whipple, a civilian medical doctor under contract to the army. He also provided medical care for the garrison at Monument Station, approximately forty-seven miles to the east. His term of service included unexpected adventures. A buffalo bull walked onto and fell through the roof of the dugout serving as Whipple's quarters. Whipple stated that the buffalo landed "in a proximity too close to be agreeable."

Another time, while returning to Pond Creek from Monument, Dr. Whipple was attacked by Indians and, while he escaped with his life, lost most of his medical supplies and private property. Fortunately the health of both garrisons was good and only one death was reported at either post during the fall and winter months. Private Thomas Hill died at Monument Station on December 5, 1865, from "wounds inflicted by Indians" on November 20.

Although battle wounds constituted a small portion of the post surgeon's attention over the years, the engagements with Indians near the post, especially in 1867 and 1868, produced a number of cases. William Bell, the Eng-

William Henry Forwood was assistant surgeon at Camp Pond Creek and Fort Wallace in March and April 1866. He was an army surgeon from 1861 until his retirement as surgeon general in 1902. He served at several frontier posts in Kansas.

Aaron Ivins Comfort served as acting assistant surgeon (a civilian contract surgeon) at Fort Wallace from August 12, 1878, to January 19, 1879.

lish physician who was at Fort Wallace during the series of Indian fights in June 1867, praised the skills of the post surgeon T. H. Turner.

> The hospital tents were crowded, and I must say that I never saw better surgery or more careful management than here, under the hands of Dr. Turner, the medical officer of the post. Two cases he was especially proud of, and certainly with reason. One was a Mexican, the other a soldier; both had been shot through the body, by an arrow. They both recovered without a bad symptom. The soldier I watched from the extraction of the arrow until he was able to walk about. The arrow had entered the back two inches from the spine, and the point had reappeared just below, and about two inches from, the navel. It had, probably, passed through the liver, without touching any other organ; still, four layers of peritoneum must have been pierced, and the recoveries, in both cases, say as much for the healthiness of the climate as for the skill of the surgeon.

Augustus Andrew De Loffre was assistant surgeon at Fort Wallace from January 3, 1881, to June 6, 1882. He was the last surgeon at the post, serving until Fort Wallace was closed. A native of France, De Loffre served as an army surgeon from 1874 until his retirement in 1899.

The surgeons at Fort Wallace generally considered the climate healthy and commented several times that the dry air seemed to facilitate the healing of wounds and some respiratory diseases. In 1867 cholera broke out along all the overland routes across Kansas and at most military posts. The Fort Wallace garrison was not so seriously affected as the Seventh Cavalry camp west of the post.

The post commander recorded at the end of July 1867 that "Cholera has made its appearance in the camp [of Seventh Cavalry west of the post] causing a considerable number of deaths daily; no cases have as yet occurred at this Post and it is expected that the desease will abate." It did the following month, but it had taken a heavy toll in the process.

In addition, during August several companies of the Fifth Infantry came to Fort Wallace from New Mexico and brought cholera with them. These soldiers were quarantined in camp about a mile west of the fort, where fourteen died. The garrison again escaped the disease, according to the post surgeon, by purifying the water supply.

Dysentery and diarrhea afflicted residents at the post. Mrs. H.C. Bankhead, wife of the post commander, saw the post surgeon on August 12 with a severe case of diarrhea from which she had suffered several days. Her illness was not given as cholera, but she died forty hours after seeing the surgeon. Colonel Bankhead exhibited similar symptoms but recovered. Diarrhea continued to be a problem in the garrison for the remainder of the summer, but no cases of cholera were diagnosed at the post.

The epidemic of Asiatic cholera that decimated soldiers and civilians along the overland trails and at several military posts and settlements in 1867 caused many more deaths than did combat with Indians. The Seventh Cavalry, for example, from its organization in 1866 to the end of 1868, lost thirty-six men in battle, six to drowning, and two missing in action. During the same period the Seventh lost fifty-one men to cholera. Fortunately, at Fort Wallace, the disease was kept out of the garrison.

In the winter and spring of 1869 Fort Wallace experienced scurvy, a disease resulting from a diet deficient in Vitamin C. This was the result of the unavailability of fresh vegetables during the winter months and a constant diet of pork. The post surgeon also blamed the frequent winter scouting expeditions with "little time intervening for purposes of recuperation." During April 1869 eighteen cases of scurvy required hospitalization, and many other soldiers suffered mild cases. Scurvy was eliminated when proper foods were provided.

In addition to diet, sanitation affected the health and comfort of the troops. The latrines were disinfected with lime regularly. Bedding could be a source of trouble. In September 1873 the post surgeon wrote that the barracks had been "so full of bedbugs" that the soldiers "slept out on the ground through the warm weather to secure rest." The following year the surgeon noted that bed ticks were washed every other month and blankets were washed twice a year. The men took their clothing to the laundress every month.

Personal hygiene was difficult at a frontier military post. Few facilities were provided for bathing during the post's early years. During the summer men could bathe in the river. In 1868 a tent for bathing was set up, with a tub for which water was heated by the laundresses. In 1874 the remodeled hospital included a room for bathing, but the post surgeon noted that the roof leaked, the sewer was plugged, and the building had neither a tub nor a stove to heat water. Even orders from the commanding officer, directing the sergeants to make certain every soldier scrubbed "the whole person" at least once a week, could not force the men to bathe when facilities were not available.

SANITATION
General Orders No. 13, April 12, 1868:
The following regulations with regard to the police of the post will be strictly observed, Company Commanders will be held responsible for the observance in all that regards the police of their Companies.

1st. All sinks will be once filled up and new trenches dug, at least eight (8) feet deep, and as narrow as practicable. They will be placed 150 yards from any barrack or inhabited building (except officers and hospital sinks)—fresh dirt to the depth of five or six inches will be thrown into the trenches every evening in warm weather and every second evening in cool weather and when they are filled to within three feet of the surface, they will be closed up and new ones dug.

2. The same distance from barracks or quarters is prescribed for cowpens and pigsties. They will be frequently cleansed, disinfected and removed. The sinks will be frequently disinfected with lime during hot weather.

3. Company Commanders will provide a large number of receptacles for Kitchen offal, will see that these do not leak, and that they are emptied frequently and disinfected with lime.

4. The Kitchens and privies will be whitewashed [with lime] on the inside once a week.

5. Every Saturday during dry weather, all bedding, clothing &ct. will be taken out of the squad rooms and thoroughly aired. Blankets will be well shaken and aired at least once a day. Bedsacks will be washed and refilled with fresh straw or hay once a month.

6. The water wagon will be washed out, scraped and thoroughly cleansed every Saturday. It will always be refilled from the dam, near the sluice, and not from the margins. Barrels for drinking purposes will be kept separate from those for laundry or other purposes, the former will be entirely inspected daily, before being refilled, will be kept covered and frequently scalded and scoured with sand. The men will be required to bathe the entire person as often as once a week. A tent for this purpose will be pitched near the laundresses and a half barrel provided. In warm weather the men will bathe in the pond prepared for their use. The foul water from the laundresses will be emptied at a distance from the barracks, and not so as to stagnate in pools. The Traders Store, cellar and surroundings will be inspected with a view to their cleanliness and sanitary condition every Saturday by the Officer of the day. All officers will see that their mess houses are kept in good condition, and that a proper disposition is made of refuse matter from them and the Company Quarters.

The problems of the Indian-fighting frontier army were many, but popular literature tends to emphasize the rigors of campaigning, the dangers of battle, and the monotony of garrison life. Health and sanitation receive little consideration, but they were crucial to the life of the soldier. The following plea written by the last commanding officer of Fort Wallace, Captain J. H. Patterson, Twentieth Infantry, to the Commissary General of Subsistence of the United States Army, February 6, 1882, portrays the daily life of the frontier soldier in a broader perspective: "I have the honor to request that 'Water Closet Paper' be provided for sale to enlisted men as it now is everything that can be used for the purpose is picked up at once, even to the premature destruction of the papers and magazines provided by the Quartermaster's Department." It would be interesting to know how much of the post library remained when the post was abandoned.

POISONING WOLVES PROHIBITED AT POST
General Orders No. 34, Dec. 17, 1868:

The sale of strychnine is hereby prohibited at this Post.
The practice of poisoning meat for the purpose of killing wolves on the military reservation is strictly forbidden.

12

Abandonment

During the early years, when Indian resistance was strong, the Fort Wallace garrison was too small to adequately protect travelers and settlers in the region. After Indians were removed from the region a few years later, the need for the post was gone. In 1870 General Pope, department commander, recommended that the garrison be reduced to a detachment to guard the buildings and supplies, keeping the post active in case it should be needed again. In 1872, when it appeared Indians were remaining on their reservations, Pope recommended that Fort Wallace be closed. He noted that the buildings were in disrepair and inadequate to quarter troops.

Even so, the post remained to help assure settlers that the region was safe. The Red River War on the Southern Plains in 1874–1875 and the fight with fleeing Cheyennes at Sappa Creek in 1875 indicated that troops were still needed on the Plains. The flight of the Northern Cheyennes under Dull Knife and Little Wolf in 1878 exemplified that need. By 1879 General Pope had decided that Fort Wallace should be expanded and made a permanent post.

He declared that of the military posts in the Central Plains, only Fort Wallace "commands all the routes by Indians to and from the Indian Territory in the south and Indian reservations north of the Platte." He recommended that quarters be built for six companies, four of cavalry and two of infantry, with sufficient storehouses for supplies required to maintain the post and send troops into the field as needed. This recom-

121

Fort Wallace at the time of its abandonment in the 1880s. At left is the commanding officer's residence, with homes of lesser officers to the right.

mendation also was disregarded. The 1878 flight of the Cheyennes proved to be the last Indian threat to Kansas settlers.

In the spring of 1882, with no apparent justification for retaining Fort Wallace, the secretary of war directed that the post be abandoned. The post officially closed May 31, 1882, but a detachment of soldiers remained to guard the buildings and prevent encroachment on the military reserve. The reservation was transferred to the Department of the Interior in July 1884.

During the spring of 1886 the remains of eighty-eight soldiers were moved from the Fort Wallace cemetery to the national cemetery at Fort Leavenworth. The civilians buried in the post cemetery were left, and this became the cemetery for the town of Wallace and surrounding area.

By 1886 settlers in the region were removing buildings or the stone and lumber from the post to use on their homesteads. The old reservation was opened to settlement in 1888, and in time all buildings at Fort Wallace were removed or destroyed. Only the cemetery site remains, with a low stone wall constructed when the post was active. A cenotaph erected in the cemetery by the Third Infantry and Seventh Cavalry to honor members of those regiments killed by Indians near the post in 1867 still stands, although the names of the soldiers incised thereon have weathered severely. Where an important military post stood from 1866 to 1882, only a few depressions and archeological artifacts remain. It is difficult to imag-

This cenotaph, erected in the Fort Wallace cemetery in 1867 to honor the soldiers of the Third Infantry and Seventh Cavalry who were killed by Indians in the vicinity, still stands inside the rock wall that was built around the post cemetery. That wall was constructed of stone from the quarry that was utilized in the construction of stone buildings erected at the fort. Although the soldiers' remains were removed to the Fort Leavenworth National Cemetery after Fort Wallace was abandoned, civilian graves remain. Beside the old post cemetery is the modern cemetery for the town of Wallace and its environs.

123

The Fort Wallace Historical Museum just east of Wallace, Kansas, includes a modern museum and the old stage station from Pond Creek.

ine the many buildings and activities at this place where history was made during the decade following the Civil War. A museum containing materials related to Fort Wallace is located near the town of Wallace.

Fort Wallace was founded to protect the Smoky Hill Trail and the railroad that replaced it as well as settlers in the region. The garrison was actively engaged in conflicts with Indians for several years, during which time Indians were forced from the area and Euro-American settlements were established. Records confirm that troops stationed at Fort Wallace, which was responsible for the defense of a large region, were engaged in more scouting expeditions, escort patrols, skirmishes, and battles with Indians than those at any other post on the central Great Plains.

Although it is popular today to criticize United States Indian policies and the role of the frontier army in the conquest of the Plains tribes, the history of Fort Wallace and the westward expansion of the nation should be judged by conditions that existed at the close of the Civil War rather than at the onset of the twenty-first century. Indians occupied land the Euro-Americans wanted. The side with population advantage and technological superiority won. What was destroyed in the process was not understood until it was too late. That is one of the tragedies of human relations. Fort Wallace is a part of the heritage of Kansas and the Great Plains. It was a part of the network of Kansas forts that helped create the society and culture we know today.

Appendix

An officer is listed for every month in which he served as commanding officer.

Captain D. C. McMichael, Thirteenth Missouri Cavalry, November 1865–February 1866

Captain Edward Ball, Second Cavalry, March–May 1866

Captain James J. Gordon, Sixth Cavalry, May–July 1866

Lieutenant Alfred Elliott Bates, Second Cavalry, July–September 1866

Lieutenant Robert E. Flood, Sixth Cavalry, September–October 1866

Lieutenant Joseph Hale, Third Infantry, October–November 1866, June–July 1867

Captain Miles W. Keogh, Seventh Cavalry, November 1866–August 1867

Captain Henry C. Bankhead, Fifth Infantry, August 1867–March 1868, July 1868–April 1869, January–April 1870, September 1870–January 1871

Captain Edmond Butler, Fifth Infantry, March, October–November 1868, January–February 1869, May–September 1870, April–October 1871

Lieutenant Colonel Charles R. Woods, Fifth Infantry, May 1869–January 1870, April–May 1870

Lieutenant Henry Romeyn, Fifth Infantry, October–November 1870

Captain James C. Casey, Fifth Infantry, January–April 1871

Colonel De Lancy Floyd-Jones, Third Infantry, October–December 1871, April–May 1872

Captain Edward Moale, Third Infantry, October 1871, December 1871–March 1872

Lieutenant Colonel John R. Brooke, Third Infantry, March–April 1872

Captain Louis T. Morris, Third Infantry, May 1872–January 1874

Captain Charles Hobart, Third Infantry, January–June 1874

Captain Howard E. Stansbury, Nineteenth Infantry, June–August 1874, May 1877

Captain Henry A. Hambright, Nineteenth Infantry, August 1874–June 1877

Lieutenant Thomas B. Robinson, Nineteenth Infantry, June–July 1875

Captain John M. Hamilton, Fifth Cavalry, July–August 1875

Lieutenant Colonel James Van Voast, Sixteenth Infantry, June–August 1877, October 1877–October 1880

Captain William G. Wedemeyer, Sixteenth Infantry, August 1877–April 1878, June 1878, March–April 1880, October–November 1880

Captain Duncan M. Vance, Sixteenth Infantry, February–June 1879, August 1879

Second Lieutenant Charles R. Tyler, Sixteenth Infantry, August–September 1880

Captain Joseph T. Haskell, Twenth–third Infantry, November 1880–October 1881

Lieutenant William C. Manning, Twenty-third Infantry, January–February 1881

Second Lieutenant George B. Read, Nineteenth Infantry, October 1881–December 1881

Captain John H. Patterson, Twentieth Infantry, December 1881–May 1882

An assistant surgeon held an appointment in the regular army. An acting assistant surgeon was a civilian who had a contract with the army to serve as a surgeon.

Acting Assistant Surgeon Whipple, November 1865–February 1866

Assistant Surgeon William Henry Forwood, March–May 1866

Acting Assistant Surgeon T. H. Turner, June 1866–July 1869 (died at the post)

Acting Assistant Surgeon E. D. Hillard, August 1867

Acting Assistant Surgeon A. W. Wiggin, October 1867–June 1868

Acting Assistant Surgeon J. A. Fitzgerald, August 1868–February 1869

Acting Assistant Surgeon John Wilson, January 1869

Acting Assistant Surgeon M. M. Shearer, July 1869–June 1871, October 1871–March 1872, June–July 1872, November 1872–January 1873

Assistant Surgeon William H. King, October 1870–October 1872, December 1872–July 1873

Acting Assistant Surgeon T. B. Chase, October–November 1872

Acting Assistant Surgeon Francis H. Atkins, July 1873–September 1874, February 1875–March 1876

Assistant Surgeon J. H. Janeway, August 1874–July 1875

Acting Assistant Surgeon A. N. Ellis, November–December 1874

Assistant Surgeon William R. Steinmetz, March 1876–September 1878

Acting Assistant Surgeon T. A. Davis, March–April 1878

Acting Assistant Surgeon Aaron Ivins Comfort, September 1878–January 1879

Assistant Surgeon James A Finley, November1878–September 1879

Acting Assistant Surgeon J. H. Page, September 1879–January 1881

Assistant Surgeon Augustus A. De Loffre, January 1881–June 1882

POST CHAPLAINS AT FORT WALLACE

William Vaux, August 1869–November 1870

George P. Van Wyck, May–September 1871

Aquila Asbury Reese, December 1871–October 1874

George A. England, November 1877, January 1878–July 1879

POST TRADERS AT FORT WALLACE

D. M. Scott, 1866–1867

Val L. Todd, 1867–1870

Homer W. Wheeler, 1870–1875

James Streeter, 1875–1876

A. W. Clark, 1876–1882

STATIONS AND DISTANCES ON THE SMOKY HILL TRAIL
JUNCTION CITY TO DENVER, 1865

Junction City to:	Miles from Station to Station	Total Miles on the Trail
Chapman's Creek	12	12
Abilene*	12	24
Solomon River	10	34
Salina*	13	47
Spring Creek	15	62
Ellsworth*	14	76
Buffalo Creek	12	88
Hick's Station*	15	102
Fossil Creek	11	113
Forsythe Creek	11	124
Big Creek*	11	135
Louisa Springs	12	147
Bluffton	14	161
Downer's Station*	13	174
Castle Rock Creek	9	183
Grannell Spring	11	194
Chalk Bluffs	12	206
Monument*	13	219
Smoky Hill Spring	11	230
Eaton*	12	242

Henshaw Creek	13	255
Pond Creek*	11	266
Willow Creek	14	280
Blue Mound	9	289
Cheyenne Wells*	13	302
Dubois*	24	326
Grady's	11	337
Cornell Creek*	13	350
Coon Creek	12	362
Hogan	11	373
Hedinger's Lake	9	382
Big Bend Sandy	13	395
Reed's Springs*	13	408
Bijou Creek	12	420
Kiowa Creek	9	429
Ruthton*	9	438
Cherry Valley	16	454
Denver	14	478

*Designates home stations where meals were served to passengers

Several changes were later made. Forsythe Creek was abandoned and a station was located at the Forks of Big Creek. Lookout Station was established west of Big Creek, and Louisa Springs was abandoned in favor of Stormy Hollow several miles farther west. Bluffton gave way to White Rock, three miles west. Willow Creek was abandoned and a new station was opened at Goose Creek, approximately ten miles west of Pond Creek.

Further Reading

Berthrong, Donald J. *The Southern Cheyennes*. Norman: University of Oklahoma Press, 1963.

Chalfant, William Y. *Cheyennes at Dark Water Creek: The Last Fight of the Red River War*. Norman: University of Oklahoma Press, 1997.

Forsyth, George A. *Thrilling Days in Army Life*. Lincoln: University of Nebraska Press, 1994.

Hoig, Stan. *The Peace Chiefs of the Cheyennes*. Norman: University of Oklahoma Press, 1980.

Leckie, William H. *The Buffalo Soldiers: A Narrative of the Negro Cavalry in the West*. Norman: University of Oklahoma Press, 1967.

Leckie, William H. *The Military Conquest of the Southern Plains*. Norman: University of Oklahoma Press, 1963.

Monnett, John H. *The Battle of Beecher Island and the Indian War of 1867–1869*. Niwot: University of Colorado Press, 1992.

Rickey, Don. *Forty Miles a Day on Beans and Hay: The Enlisted Soldier Fighting the Indian Wars*. Norman: University of Oklahoma Press, 1963.

Stallard, Patricia Y. *Glittering Misery: Dependents of the Indian Fighting Army*. Norman: University of Oklahoma Press, 1992.

Utley, Robert M. *Frontier Regulars: The United States Army and the Indian, 1866–1891*. New York: Macmillan Publishing Co., 1973.

Utley, Robert M., ed. *Life in Custer's Cavalry: Diaries and Letters of Albert and Jennie Barnitz, 1867–1868*. New Haven: Yale University Press, 1977.

Wheeler, Homer W. *Buffalo Days*. Lincoln: University of Nebraska Press, 1990.

Acknowledgments

The author wishes to thank the following individuals for their help, information, and encouragement in the preparation of this history: Stephanie Brock, William Y. Chalfant, Virgil W. Dean, George Elmore, Douglas Hurt, Harry C. Myers, Thomas Railsback, Dave Webb, and Wilbur Williams. The assistance and courtesy of the personnel at the following institutions was invaluable and is gratefully acknowledged: the National Archives, the U.S. Army Military History Institute, and the Kansas State Historical Society. My wife, Bonita, assisted with the research and assumed extra responsibilities so I could devote time to this project.

Illustration Credits

All illustrations are from the collections of the Kansas State Historical Society, with the following exceptions: facing title page courtesy Illinois State Historical Library; 18, 19 National Archives; 26 Kenneth J. Almy; 33, 34 (bottom), 36 Kansas Collection, University of Kansas Libraries; 49 Colorado Historical Society; 54, 55 Yale Collection of Western Americana, Beinecke Library, Yale University; 60 Library of Congress; 75, 78 (bottom), 80 Denver Public Library, Western History Department; 99, 100 Department of the Army, U.S. Military History Institute; 106 Thomas Railsback and the Old Guard Museum; 110, 111 Department of the Army, U.S. Military History Institute; 114 Kansas Collection, University of Kansas Libraries.

This publication has been financed in part with federal funds from the National Park Service, a division of the United States Department of the Interior, and administered by the Kansas State Historical Society. The contents and opinions, however, do not necessarily reflect the views or policies of the United States Department of the Interior or the Kansas State Historical Society.

This program receives federal financial assistance. Under Title VI of the Civil Rights Act of 1964, Section 504 of the Rehabilitation Act of 1973, and the Age Discrimination Act of 1975, as amended, the United States Department of the Interior prohibits discrimination on the basis of race, color, national origin, disability, or age in its federally assisted programs. If you believe you have been discriminated against in any program, activity, or facility as described above, or if you desire further information, please write to: Office of Equal Opportunity, National Park Service, P.O. Box 37127, Washington, D.C. 20013–7127.